COLORADO SPAS

45 Rejuvenating Retreats

COLORADO SPAS

45 Rejuvenating Retreats

KALPANA G. MUETZ & KRISTI L. FRUSH

WITH JILLIAN LAVIGNE

FULCRUM
GOLDEN, COLORADO

Library of Congress Cataloging-in-Publication Data
Muetz, Kalpana G.
  Colorado spas : 45 rejuvenating retreats / Kalpana G. Muetz and
Kristi
L. Frush with Jillian LaVigne.
    p. cm.
  ISBN 978-1-55591-640-4 (pbk.)
  1. Health resorts--Colorado--Guidebooks. I. Frush, Kristi L. II.
LaVigne, Jillian. III. Title.
  RA807.C59M84 2009
  613'.12209788--dc22

Printed on recycled paper in Canada by Friesens Corp.

0 9 8 7 6 5 4 3 2 1

Design by Jack Lenzo
Map by Marge Mueller, Gray Mouse Graphics

Fulcrum Publishing
4690 Table Mountain Drive, Suite 100
Golden, Colorado 80403
800-992-2908 • 303-277-1623
www.fulcrumbooks.com

To those who strive for balance in your busy lives: remember to take time out for yourself to reconnect to your well-being.

To our family and friends, who have supported and encouraged us throughout this endeavor.

And to each other, for the different perspectives and contributions we each brought to this project.

CONTENTS

FOREWORD

We began this project with the goal of expanding spa choices for those who live in and travel to Colorado. Each of us has found our way to spas for varying reasons. Kristi believes in going to the spa for stress relief and pampering, to combat the effects of her busy life. For Jillian, spa-going is about increased focus, memory, and the mind-body connection. And Kalpana's visits to spas enable her to continue the traditions of Eastern thought and balance in her life. Our hope for you, our readers, is that you will find spas that fit each of you individually.

To make navigating the spas of Colorado easier for you, this book is divided into five regions: North Central, Front Range, West Central, South Central, and Southwest. Our selection of 45 spas includes an eclectic range of day, destination, and resort venues. We chose these entries based on each spa's level of customer service, cleanliness, location, mission and philosophy, community service, types of offerings, and our overall experience.

Throughout the book, you will find the following icons. These features may further assist you in locating a spa with the right qualities for you.

$ Bargain ($75 or less for a 50-minute service)

$$ Moderate/reasonably priced ($76–$100 for a 50-minute service)

$$$ Indulgent ($101 or more for a 50-minute service)

Fitness facility (Often includes exercise equipment and yoga/Pilates, occasionally includes a swimming pool)

Lunch/dining options

Hot springs/soaking facilities

Overnight accommodations

Family friendly (The whole family is either welcome to the spa or there are things for children to do while parents enjoy the spa)

Romantic getaway

At the end of the book, you will find a glossary of spa terms as well as a guide to spa etiquette and spa trends. These should help familiarize the novice spa-goer to the spa-going experience and help make your time at the spa more comfortable.

Our purpose is to provide you with ideas of what to expect during your visits. Be aware that each spa's services may change often, so it is best to explore a spa's website ahead of time or call the spa for more information and help in finding the right treatment for you. Our descriptions are based on our own experiences, but it is important to note that each person's spa experience will be different.

Be sure to bring this book along with you as you travel to a spa. Many of the spas included here offer special discounts for first-time visitors. But please note that in order to receive these discounts, you must refer to the book when you schedule your appointment. Certain restrictions apply. Please inquire at each spa.

Our wish is that you will not only see more of the state while you are traveling to different spas, but also experience a variety of treatments that can help you feel better both physically and mentally along the way. But whatever your reason for going to the spa, we hope this book helps you find what you are looking for.

INTRODUCTION
ORIGINS

Throughout history, the use of healing waters can be seen in depictions of early cultures. In Babylonian, Greek, and Roman times, people were often portrayed immersing themselves in therapeutic pools. Since the time of the Romans, the Belgian town of Spa has been known for its baths, and many people think this is the origin of the word *spa* we use today.

The popularity of spas has waxed and waned over time. In the 19th century, great spa destinations were frequented by the wealthy in Europe, but with the surge of medical discoveries in the 20th century, spas and healing waters were no longer at the forefront of how people took care of themselves. Today, a new focus on relaxation, wellness, and pampering has led to a resurgence of spa-goers enjoying the benefits of heat, water, and massage once again.

In Colorado, the history of the spa dates back to Native Americans and pioneers who discovered the numerous hot springs that are found here. People travel from far and wide to partake in the gifts of these healing waters.

We met with Roland McCook, a Native American representative for the Smithsonian and the great-great-grandson of Chief Ouray, at the

Ute Indian Museum in Montrose. McCook generously provided us with some history on Colorado's natural springs. Chief Ouray and his wife, Chipeta, spent many years in Colorado during the 1800s. The grounds of The Historic Wiesbaden Hot Springs Spa and Lodgings (page 154) were once the hunting lodge and retreat of Chief Ouray.

The Noochew, the original name of the Ute Indians, are a nomadic people who trust that the spirits live among us. The Noochew feel that Mother Earth provided the hot springs as a sacred place for meditation. McCook described how the Noochew believe that they are standing in the footsteps of those who came before them. Many of the spas in Colorado are linked to springs and vapor caves that represent sacred places for the Ute Indians. These precious waters are still used for prayer and meditation by the Ute people.

Whether you visit with friends and loved ones or seek a more contemplative, solitary retreat, we hope you enjoy knowing the historical significance of these revered sites.

MAP

MAP 1

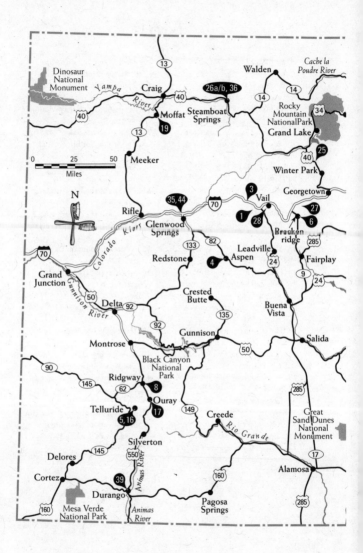

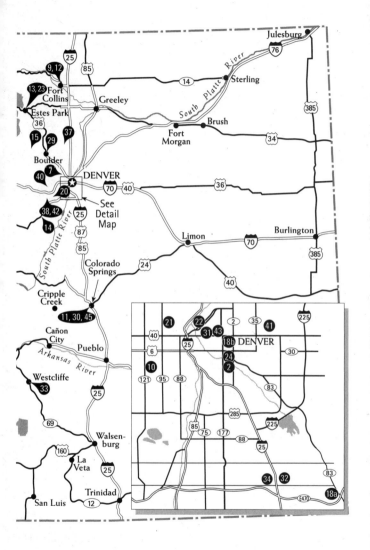

Julesburg

⟨76⟩

⟨25⟩ ⟨85⟩

9, 12

⟨14⟩ South Platte River Sterling

13, 23 Fort Collins

Greeley ⟨385⟩

Estes Park

⟨36⟩ 37 Brush

15 29 Fort Morgan ⟨34⟩

Boulder

7

40 DENVER ⟨70⟩ ⟨40⟩ ⟨36⟩ ⟨385⟩

20

See Detail Map

38, 42 ⟨25⟩ Burlington

14 ⟨87⟩ Limon ⟨70⟩

South Platte River ⟨85⟩

Colorado Springs ⟨24⟩ ⟨40⟩

Cripple Creek

11, 30, 45

Cañon City

Arkansas River Pueblo

Westcliffe

33

⟨25⟩

⟨69⟩

⟨160⟩ Walsenburg

La Veta ⟨25⟩

San Luis Trinidad ⟨12⟩

Detail Map:

21 22 ⟨2⟩ ⟨35⟩ 41 ⟨225⟩

31 43 18b DENVER

⟨40⟩ ⟨25⟩ ⟨30⟩

⟨6⟩ 24

2

10 ⟨83⟩

⟨121⟩ ⟨95⟩ ⟨88⟩

⟨285⟩ ⟨225⟩

⟨85⟩ ⟨75⟩ ⟨177⟩ ⟨88⟩

⟨25⟩

34 32 ⟨83⟩

E470 18a

MAP 3

NORTH CENTRAL

<u>STEAMBOAT SPRINGS</u>

The Rocky Mountain Day Spa

5th St. and Lincoln Ave. • Steamboat Springs, CO 80477

970-870-9860 • www.steamboatmassage.com

2220 Village Inn Ct. • Steamboat Springs, CO 80477

970-871-6111 • www.steamboatmassage.com

*If you look for quality in ambiance,
people, and services, The Rocky Mountain
Day Spa is the place for you.*

Located in the northwest part of the state, Steamboat Springs is known for its friendly people, incredible skiing, summer fun, and cultural offerings. The town is named for its natural mineral springs, which were discovered by pioneers in the 1800s. It is said that a *chug* sound could be heard coming from these waters before a train track was laid over them, hence the name *Steamboat*. The Ute Indians were the first to use these springs. They were later followed by gold miners, and eventually many others who traveled here to experience the springs' healing properties.

In the heart of downtown Steamboat Springs, just off 5th St. and Lincoln Ave., resides The Rocky Mountain Day Spa, a local favorite. This elegant and serene spa leaves nothing to be desired. The artistic touches of owner Seana Cardillo invite customers to reach a level of serenity in a modern, elegant setting with which most other spas cannot compete. From the intricate stone candleholders to the unique pedicure bowls, Cardillo has set the scene for an impeccable day at the spa. The calming brown and beige hues, along with these little details in the decor, provide spa-goers with a seamless transition to a state of tranquility.

Cardillo's warm and giving personality creates a feeling at The Rocky Mountain Day Spa that cannot be duplicated elsewhere. Her family of therapists exemplifies the principles of nurturing care through their outpouring of kindness and compassion. Whether it is your first visit or your hundredth, you can expect to be treated as though you are invaluable. A service here is truly something that you will have to experience for yourself.

The Euphoric Eucalyptus treatment lasts an hour and a half and is worth every cent of the price. First, fresh eucalyptus leaves, used for detoxification, are meticulously placed on one side of your body. Then you are treated to a soothing rosemary-jojoba hot-oil scalp massage. When the leaves are removed, be prepared for an extensive hot-stone massage. Just when you think the treatment has ended, it begins again on the other side of your body. When it is all over, you will leave feeling like royalty.

A specialty at The Rocky Mountain Day Spa is Ashiatsu Oriental bar therapy. During this treatment, a therapist uses her feet to create a deep-tissue massage on the client while holding on to an apparatus above. Jackie Braley, who is skilled in this type of massage, explained the origins and benefits of Ashiatsu. The technique was created by Ruthie Piper Hardee, a Denver resident, and was the first of its kind to be approved by the National Certification Board for Therapeutic Massage & Bodywork. Although it sounds intimidating, there is nothing to be afraid of—because of the way the bars are used, the therapist can control the pressure and simultaneously offer you a type of relief that you can't find anywhere else. This treatment is highly recommended.

The rich array of excellent services available also includes facials, reflexology, body scrubs, body wraps, Reiki, and massage. An additional highlight is the multihead Cascade Steam Shower, which beckons spa-goers with an added form of relief.

Men and women, locals and travelers, all enjoy the many offerings here. It is easy to see why The Rocky Mountain Day Spa is the preferred spa of many local resorts.

When in town, live like the locals do and treat yourself to a spa experience that will transform your mind, body, and soul.

A second location can be found at the Sheraton Resort on the mountain.

- Featured treatments: Euphoric Eucalyptus, Ashiatsu Massage
- 10% discount
- Hours: Mon.–Sat. 9:00 AM–7:00 PM

The Rocky Mountain Day Spa

Strawberry Park Hot Springs

44200 CR 36 • Steamboat Springs, CO 80487

970-879-0342 • www.strawberryhotsprings.com

*Something wonderful cascades down a
mountainside in Steamboat…Make your
way to Strawberry Park Hot Springs.*

Strawberry Park Hot Springs is located only
seven miles outside of Steamboat Springs.
Here, you will find hot springs and a few cooler
pools to soak, play, and relax in. The springs
lie between Rocky Peak and Cooper Ridge. The
pools are of various sizes and kept at different
temperatures to accommodate the needs of many
visitors, although the average temperature is
approximately 150°F.

Strawberry Park has beautiful waterfalls
and a lovely steam room, but keep in mind that
although this is a wonderful experience, it is a
rustic one. For example, some of the changing
rooms do not have doors. There is a teepee in
which to change as well, but many people don't
knock before entering. This is a family friendly
location during the day, but if you are planning
on visiting at night, throw off your bathing suit,
as clothes are optional after dark.

Don Johnson has been the owner for about 25 years. The decor and architecture that you see are based on his vision, which is earthy yet contemporary. The Ute Indians used to live in the area and found the springs to be healing. You can still feel the spiritual aura of these blessed grounds. There is an intense fire that fuels and energizes the water that spills down the hill.

Strawberry Park offerings include many Eastern techniques, such as craniosacral, Reiki, and raindrop therapy, as well as the more familiar deep-tissue and sports massages. One of the most requested services is Watsu. Watsu is a form of aquatic therapy that incorporates techniques from Zen Shiatsu, a method of movement and stretching from Japan. The therapist connects the movements with the breath of the person having the treatment. He or she does not hurry the process or lead the client into a faster pace, but instead is one with the client, individualizing the process along the way. The purpose of Watsu is to free, or release, the body in the water. When you are in the water and become relaxed, you become buoyant and the water supports you completely. The tissues in your body expand, creating more space, because of the lack of gravity.

Experiencing a water massage in this environment is exhilarating. Two floatation braces are put on your legs, and you lie back in the therapist's arms in 96°F to 99°F water. During this time, you will find that trust is a great virtue. You are embraced and led through currents of relaxing rhythms as the therapist guides you from side to side.

When you visit Strawberry Park, bring a picnic, as well as lots of water to prevent dehydration. Come with the family, escape with some friends, or get away by yourself to soak in these amazing streams of well-being.

- Featured treatment: Watsu
- 10% discount
- Hours: Sun.–Thurs. 10:00 AM 10:30 PM,
  Fri. & Sat. 10:00 AM–12:00 AM

Strawberry Park Hot Springs

Ranch Creek Spa

Devil's Thumb Ranch • 3530 CR 83 • Tabernash, CO 80478

800-933-4339 • www.devilsthumbranch.com

$$$ 🛏️

If you want to enjoy the tranquil beauty of Colorado in a state-of-the-art spa, visit the Ranch Creek Spa at Devil's Thumb Ranch.

Three miles off Hwy. 40 in Tabernash, and just 15 minutes from Winter Park, you will find the Ranch Creek Spa at Devil's Thumb Ranch. The ranch encompasses 5,000 acres, so be prepared to find yourself in awe. The scenery is so enticing and welcoming it is hard not to leave all your cares behind.

The Ute and Arapaho tribes who settled their differences in the Ranch Creek Valley are said to have named Devil's Thumb. According to legend, they buried the devil but left his thumb exposed to remind them of the evils of war. His thumb is visible as a rock formation on top of the Continental Divide.

Devil's Thumb has existed as a guest ranch for nearly 60 years. Its mission is to create a unique and authentic Colorado experience for guests that honors the outdoors, the beautiful natural resources, and the rugged individualism that is the hallmark of the West.

The interior of the Ranch Creek Spa is very inviting. It is decorated in rich, warm colors that enhance the overall peaceful atmosphere. The spa is housed in a geothermally powered 10,000-square-foot building in a quiet corner of a meadow. There are eight treatment rooms, a 700-square-foot couple's suite, a yoga lookout studio, and separate men's and women's facilities. There is even an aromatherapy room, steam room, and sauna.

Faye Hutchins, spa manager, described the special extras that are added to services, including such niceties as hot towels, foot balm, and a cool eye pillow. Yoga classes are available; participating in one can be a great way to begin a day at the spa. It is easy to draw connections between practicing yoga and the spa experience. When one surrenders to the practice of the asanas (which means "poses"), the experience is deepened and you are able to reap the true benefits of yoga, just as surrendering to a spa treatment can allow you to get the most from it.

A specialty here is a hot infused-towel massage. It begins with an essential-oil massage. Next, hot, steaming towels that are steeped in aromatic essences are used for more massage in order to initiate sweating and the detoxifying process. The service concludes with a light massage done through a sheet on both the back and front sides of the body.

Additional favorites include the soaking tubs, which are available in some treatment rooms. Guests also have access to the heated indoor and outdoor pools and hot tubs. In the outdoor soaking pool, a waterfall from above allows you to position your neck and shoulders in a way that deepens the effects of the therapeutic splash.

Additional activities at Devil's Thumb Ranch include snowshoeing, fly-fishing, rafting, kayaking, hiking, mountain biking, and swimming.

Like the naturally flowing creek, purposeful in its direction, the Ranch Creek Spa provides an authentic sense of peace, allowing each guest to explore the land while embarking on a personal journey to reveal his or her new self.

- Featured treatments: Hot Towel Infused Massage, Invigorating Soak
- 10% discount
- Hours: Mon.–Fri. 10:00 AM–5:00 PM, Sat. & Sun. 9:00 AM–6:00 PM

The Parlour Salon and Spa at the Stanley Hotel

333 E. Wonderview Ave. • Estes Park, CO 80517

970-586-9250 • www.theparlour.net/estes.html

*If you are looking for a spa that makes
the whole world revolve around you,
The Parlour Salon and Spa
is the place to go.*

Pour yourself a thermos of a hot beverage, grab your camera, and head west on Hwy. 34 from Grand Lake. Traveling over Trail Ridge Rd., it should take you only about an hour to reach Estes Park, but allow yourself plenty of time to enjoy the drive. You may even want to stop to take in the view of the cliffs and appreciate the grandeur of the Rocky Mountains.

The Parlour at the Stanley Hotel, which comprises both a salon and spa, strives to become your refuge from the busy world. It is part of a chain of six salons, but it's the first one to incorporate a day spa. There are several treatment rooms, and the menu offers choices ranging from skin care to individual and couple's massages, as well as other body treatments and packages. The spa caters to large groups, especially wedding parties.

The salon is located at the front of the spa and has an upbeat feel, great natural light, and numerous products for purchase. In contrast, the spa is calm and inviting—the lights are dim and the room is infused with the scent of vanilla candles, the sight of soothing colors, and the sounds of classical music. The spa appears simple and quiet, and the comfortable, old-fashioned furniture beckons you to stay and unwind.

It is clear that the therapists at the Parlour care about customer service and the client experience. A special blend of fresh herbs and minerals is mixed into all of their oils, creams, and sugar and salt scrubs for an added custom touch. The ancient therapy of hot-stone massage is a specialty here. The heat from the stones penetrates deep into the layers of your muscles. This is an especially effective way to dissolve built-up tension in your shoulders, neck, and back.

The 60-minute Arctic Algae Mineral Wrap is another favorite. It will detoxify, regenerate, and revitalize you while replacing lost minerals. First, a nutrient-rich layer of Arctic algae seaweed is applied to your body. The micronutrients in the algae penetrate your skin and increase your circulation. Next, you will enjoy a relaxing private shower. This is then followed by a hydrating cream to complete your experience.

The Manicure-and-Pedicure Combination is far beyond a basic service. It begins with a cooling soak of your hands, followed by nail shaping, cuticle trimming, and exfoliation. The manicure is completed with a moisture-rich lotion application and the nail polish color of your choice. The pedicure begins with a Jacuzzi foot soak and includes cuticle care, exfoliation, moisture, and polish, all experienced from the comfort of your heated throne/massage chair.

- Featured treatments: Hot Stones Therapy, Arctic Algae Mineral Wrap, Manicure-and-Pedicure Combination
- 10% discount
- Hours: Daily 10:00 AM–6:00 PM

The Parlour Salon and Spa

Elements of Touch Wellness Spa & River Retreat

477 Pine River Ln. • Estes Park, CO 80517

970-586-6597 • www.estesriverretreat.com

$

Are you ready to slow down and find deep inner peace? If so, Elements of Touch is where you need to be.

At Elements of Touch Wellness Spa & River Retreat, expect to indulge in one of the coziest and most relaxing retreats in Colorado. The entrance lies alongside the Big Thompson River and is nestled in a bank of trees and flowers. The spa is light, open, and welcoming. Original artwork adorns the walls, and powerful quotes are found in frames throughout. Enjoy a cup of organically grown Estes Park coffee while you soak in the tub and reinvent yourself. Or wander outside—a wicker chair sitting next to the river invites you to enjoy the scenery.

In existence since 1992, a recent expansion has allowed the spa to offer additional services. There are three treatment rooms, shower facilities, and even on-site luxury lodging. The Estes River Retreat, for example, is a beautiful vacation home that you can reserve all to yourself. It includes three bedrooms that can accommodate up to six guests, a full kitchen, and more. The spa has also introduced yoga, Pilates, and core classes to its menu of offerings. There is a hairstylist across the street who works with clients of Elements of Touch, so make sure to add on a hair treatment if you would like one to follow your spa service.

Elements of Touch offers bodywork services for those who are suffering from chronic pain and daily aching joints, as well as for those who are looking for progressive forms of relaxation. The spa offers a wellness menu that gives your body, mind, and spirit the opportunity to relax, detox, and return to a life renewed. Therapists will even work with physicians and other medical teams to best benefit clients.

The Glacial Meltdown is a particular specialty. It includes a full-body massage, salt glow for your back, and foot and hand treatments. It is deep and thorough and two hours long. You will be lavishly pampered.

The Rocky Mountain High, another signature of Elements of Touch, is also recommended. It includes a salt glow, hot shower, and hot-oil full-body lymphatic massage, which is not to be missed. This massage will help boost your immune system, eliminate toxins, increase your metabolism, and beckon you into deep relaxation.

Owner Ravit Michener has created a sanctuary. You will feel that you are in good hands here, as Michener's work is described by regulars as exquisite.

- Featured treatments: Glacial Meltdown, Rocky Mountain High
- 10% discount
- Hours: Please call

Front Range

Fort Collins

Cleopatra's Day Spa

1435 S. College Ave. • Fort Collins, CO 80524

970-221-0506 • www.fortcollinsdayspa.com

Want to feel at home at the spa?
Try Cleopatra's Day Spa.

When driving from Estes Park to Fort Collins, you will be amazed at the vast open space that still exists. While developing neighborhoods are on the rise, this agricultural area can still boast of small-town charm. Acclaimed as one of the best places to live in the United States, Fort Collins offers a high quality of life.

Cleopatra's Day Spa is on the northwest corner of Prospect Rd. and College Ave., not far from Colorado State University or downtown Fort Collins. It is in a converted old home that was built in 1910. It is comfortable, warm, and inviting. A regal picture of Cleopatra greets you in the cozy reception area, which is drenched in warm purple and gold. Each of the six treatment rooms is uniquely decorated with an infusion of color, and small touches have been added to create the feeling of an escape. The green tropical room, for example, treats clients to natural light during the day and relaxes them with candlelight in the evening. All aspects tell you that this day spa is like no other and you will feel at home immediately. From the hospitality you receive when making your first phone call through the ambiance you experience while receiving treatments, you feel like you are being given a warm hug.

Cleopatra's strives to become the area's first choice when it comes time for a little pampering. A variety of well-trained staff are on hand to serve clients. They are continually adding the latest in treatments so you can be sure to receive the most beneficial services available. Cleopatra's stresses the healthy long-term benefits of preventive therapies. The spa's owner, Janet Rossi Sanders, describes Cleopatra's as "a therapeutic haven for overworked, stressed moms and dads, college students, business professionals, outdoor enthusiasts, and adventure seekers—a place to unwind and feel protected and nurtured."

To give yourself hours to unwind and sample a selection of the services offered, try a package like Cleopatra's Day Off. It begins with a Swedish massage, followed by the Eminence Custom Facial, then the Citrus Lip Treatment, and ends with the Classic Pedicure. The Swedish massage is done with long massage strokes and is best for those seeking both relaxation and improved circulation. The Eminence Custom Facial is an all-organic facial treatment that includes massaging the neck, shoulders, arms, and hands. The Citrus Lip Treatment provides moisture and exfoliation—and it tastes great and makes your lips plump! The Classic Pedicure is done with a sugar scrub to remove dry skin and includes soaking, cuticle care, and nail polish.

Another favorite of Cleopatra's clients are the body treatments. The Milk-and-Honey Wrap quenches dry Colorado skin. You will be cocooned in a fairly tight wrap while a milk-and-honey sugar polish penetrates deeply into the layers of your skin. A shower and soothing organic-product application top off this hour-and-a-half-long refreshing treatment.

Cleopatra's has been in business for 11 years. Not only does this spa have a lot of experience, it also has a spacious room to host large parties and cater in food for lunch.

When leaving the spa, you will be told to "breathe deep, smile, and relax. Use the slow lane driving, and don't turn on the television when you get home."

- Featured treatments: Cleopatra's Day Off, The Milk-and-Honey Wrap
- Hours: Mon.–Fri. 10:00 AM–5:00 PM, Sat. 9:00 AM–4:00 PM

Elements Rejuvenating Day Spa

2008 E. Harmony Rd. • Fort Collins, CO 80528

970-377-9868 • www.elements-dayspa.com

Revive at Elements Rejuvenating Day Spa.

Less than three miles from I-25, Elements Rejuvenating Day Spa sits at the northwest corner of Harmony Dr. and Timberline Rd. With restaurants and movie theaters just across the street, it is in a great location. From the outside the spa looks like a small green house, but inside you will not believe the sophistication of your surroundings.

At the door, light music and the soothing aroma of this Eastern paradise greet you. There are separate very aesthetically pleasing areas for manicures and pedicures, lunch, and treatments. The reception room includes chairs and a couch for your relaxation, and a collection of products for you to browse. The Tea Room is more secluded and a peaceful place in which to sit before services. There are sections of the spa with knotty pine walls and ceilings that make it feel like a cozy log home. This rustic feeling is balanced with elegant Asian influences in the decor and the uniforms worn by the therapists.

Owner Thanya Nguyen does an incredible job of managing the business and providing comprehensive services for her clients. Her philosophy is to keep the every need and want of the customer in mind. Healing, which is based on the whole person and the interrelationship of people with their natural surroundings, is done by balancing the five elements: water, fire, earth, metal, and wood. Nguyen wants her customers to remember that when they enter the spa, it is their time. She works hard to ensure that every comfort is extended to them so they feel like they are away from their busy lives.

There are 16 therapists on staff. They work to help their clients restore balance, find a sense of well-being, and relieve stress. Customers describe them as calm, soothing, knowledgeable, and down-to-earth. Many clients are regulars. You might wish you could stay all night, as the spa feels a lot like a second home where you can just toss off your shoes and make yourself comfortable.

This spa has an environment that appeals to both men and women, and it is clear that both sexes are at ease here. Indeed, Elements attracts a variety of clients, from couples to mothers to students and professionals. The spa also offers services for parties or corporate gatherings of 2 to 20 people, for which the staff can arrange to include a formal, catered-in lunch.

Elements offers all-day packages that include facials, wraps, massages, and nail care. Some creative treatments are offered as well, including the Rose Petal Massage, a 60-minute massage where the fragrance of rose petals is not only in the oils, but also all around you.

The Couple's Room at Elements is one of a kind. Up the stairs, in a loft area, a glorious room awaits. There are window seats for each of you and enough space and seclusion to enjoy your shared experience. Each person can choose from the various massages offered, allowing for a custom and couple's experience simultaneously. The lucky husband who was able to come along for this service said that it was the best massage he has ever had.

- Featured treatments: Couple's Massage, Rose Petal Massage
- 10% discount
- Hours: Mon. & Sat. 9:00 AM–5:00 PM, Tues.–Fri. 10:00 AM–7:00 PM

Sunflower Spa

1700 Kylie Dr., Ste. 150 • Longmont, CO 80501

303-485-1390 • www.everyoneblooms.com

$

*Dreaming of a spa that specializes
in custom care? Look no further than
the Sunflower Spa.*

Just a few minutes off I-25 and Hwy. 119, a picture-perfect spa awaits you. Sunflower Spa is one that we don't just recommend visiting—you might want to move closer to it! Oh, what these lucky Longmont residents have right at their fingertips. This spa is not missing a thing. On the border of a residential neighborhood, this easy-to-find two-year-old spa is just beautiful. From the brick exterior to your first step inside the door, it is easy to see that this will be a quality experience in every way.

Owner Patrice von Metzger worked in human resources for 15 years. Then, after an extensive five-year search for a business venture, she decided to combine her love of people with her love of spas. An avid spa-goer, she has infused the best of her own spa experiences into this delightful day spa. Her expertise at working with people is evident in the friendly approach of her staff and therapists toward clients. Newcomers are provided with a comprehensive questionnaire that helps determine skin tone, massage pressure preferences, and more. Massage therapists like Crystal Clark take time to listen to your needs and create incredible services. And the staff works hard to remember all of their customers, whether they come in twice a year or once a month.

An array of jewelry and spa products lines the brightly painted walls of the spa entryway, and the sunflower theme is visible throughout. The uplifting and positive hues are excellently balanced with serene and elegant decor. There are full-service locker rooms, complete with amenities such as steam rooms and showers for men and women—and, indeed, both men and women are comfortable here. In fact, a treatment in the expansive couple's room would make for a great date. There are a lot of places to sit and wait for services throughout the spa, and in the designated waiting area guests will find water, tea, and reading material for their enjoyment.

Sunflower offers a creative website from which gift certificates can be immediately downloaded and tailored in design and denomination to meet your needs. Sunflower's unique touch is also visible in the custom-blended massage oils, scrubs, and body butters that are used on clients, and in the steam and Swiss shower body treatments, which surpass all expectations.

You might want to try an Exotic Destination service for your next manicure, pedicure, massage, or body treatment. You can choose from three essences: Moroccan rose, Tunisian neroli, or Malaysian silk. After you've chosen your destination, one of the services you can enjoy is the Exotic Paradise Body Treatment, which begins with a warm oil massage for the scalp and hair, hands, feet, and body. An exotic sugar scrub is then heated and gently worked into the skin with warm stones. The treatment concludes with a warm Swiss steam shower, completing a day of perfect self-indulgence.

Sunflower Spa is a place you will want to come time and time again for a rejuvenating and relaxing experience.

- Featured treatments: Exotic Paradise...
  An Exotic Destination Service
- 10% discount
- Hours: Tue.–Fri. 9:00 AM–8:00 PM,
  Sat. 9:00 AM–6:00 PM, Sun. 10:00 AM–5:00 PM

The Spa at St. Julien

900 Walnut St. • Boulder, CO 80302

877-303-0900 • www.stjulien.com

*Want a getaway but don't want to travel
far from Denver? St. Julien in Boulder has
the spa for you. Whether you stay overnight
at the hotel or escape to the spa for the day,
you will never want to leave.*

The professional yet relaxed atmosphere that emanates from St. Julien represents the essence of Colorado. Not pretentious in any way, the only destination spa in Boulder adds special touches to treatments, including rose petals under the face cradle during massage services and hot towels, water, and fruit to refresh you afterward. The spa uses indigenous plants and stones in the creation of products used in their unique services. These amenities, combined with the decor and friendliness of the staff, create a tranquil and soothing environment.

The Spa at St. Julien continues to grow as a world-class spa while maintaining a community- and eco-friendly consciousness. The hotel features more than 200 rooms and has a business center, fitness center, and a 60-foot indoor lap pool. The 10,000-square-foot spa features 12 treatment rooms and a separate salon area, and guests are free to use the great steam room and huge hot tub before or after treatments. Guests also have complimentary access to the pool, fitness area, and locker rooms. There may be even more to look forward to in the future—the spa director, Candis Ayers, plans to promote yoga classes soon. This will reinforce the idea that visiting the spa can be a healthy lifestyle habit rather than just a day to indulge.

The Spa at St. Julien offers an extensive menu that includes signature spa packages, body treatments, massages with international flair, and salon services. If you are having problems choosing, let us recommend the Boulder Rocks. This treatment will cater to your indecision by pampering you with both a hot-stone massage and a gemstone facial. At a little over two hours long, this treatment stands alone. A cleansing and moisturizing facial integrates chakra balancing with the alignment of gemstones. The therapist performing the full-body hot-stone massage never loses focus. As she uses the stones as a resource and tool, you are provided with the full benefits of their healing properties. Not only does the expertise of the therapist make you feel at ease, but the massage-and-facial combination will penetrate any stress barriers you may have arrived with. As the tension melts, everything else around you fades away. You may soon forget that the therapist is in the room with you. In fact, you might even forget that *you* are in the room!

Go all out and treat yourself to the Cocktail Pedicure afterward, enjoying your favorite drink while extending the relaxation process. Your feet will be treated to a soak, exfoliation, moisturizing mask, and paraffin dip before the polish. At the end, your feet and toes will thank you.

After a day at the spa, enjoy lunch on the terrace while taking in the beauty of the surrounding Flatirons. Amid the urban atmosphere, you will be transported to a place where your list of things to do no longer matters.

- Featured treatments: Boulder Rocks, Cocktail Pedicure
- 10% discount on three or more services
- Hours: Daily 9:00 AM–8:00 PM

The Spa at St. Julien

Gold Lake Mountain Resort and Spa

3371 Gold Lake Rd. • Ward, CO 80481

800-450-3544 • www.goldlake.com

$$\$\$\$$

*Escape to an early-1900s
cabin retreat where the elements
of nature create a peaceful escape.*

Not far from Boulder or Nederland is the town of Ward, where you will find an uplifting spa experience at Gold Lake. In the mid-1800s, Gold Lake offered local Indian tribes a gathering place to celebrate annual festivities and engage in peaceful dialogue. In 1861, the establishment of the Gold Lake mining district drove the tribes away. A dam was built at the southern end of the lake, and the town of Gold Lake was plotted. Fortunately, gold was never found in this area, and to this day it maintains its appeal as a peaceful escape. After the turn of the century, Gold Lake went through many phases as tourists from Nederland flocked to Estes Park on the Peak to Peak Scenic and Historic Byway. Featuring 19 cabins, Gold Lake now serves as a rustic yet upscale mountain spa and resort. An exceptional location for retreats and celebrations, it offers guests a tranquil and transcendental experience.

Gold Lake is currently undergoing a facial itself. Managing partners Shelley Kappel and David Brand are recultivating the grounds to honor the sacredness on which Gold Lake was originally founded. Both Native American and Eastern techniques are used in treatments to spiritually cleanse the land as well as help guests transform to better health.

Although we visited Gold Lake on a rainy autumn day, none of the beauty of this area was lost. You may have a difficult time getting cell phone service here, but don't worry—you will not want technology interfering with your escape. The environment you are surrounded by is warm, inviting, and spiritually uplifting. In a very *Walden*-esque way, you can envision yourself having a conversation with Thoreau about living in the moment. Relax in the Sage Room of the spa and enjoy a cup of tea as you take in the spectacular view of the lake.

The staff is extremely friendly and accommodating. The spa director, Jennifer Arnone, creates personalized formulations from the local herbs and flowers that activate the healing essences of each plant. The spa uses Pangaea Organics and Annaé Geoceuticals, both local products from Boulder. There are many treatments to choose from, including Eastern-inspired therapies, energy-based work, hot-stone reflexology, gemstone facials, and the Rocky Mountain Clay Body Wrap.

Raindrop therapy uses drops of nine essential oils along your spine to help decrease inflammation. (Be sure to inquire about the oils that are used in case of sensitive skin or allergic reactions.) During this massage, the therapist was very tuned in to my needs; she seemed to have magical hands that sent energy wherever my body needed it. As your skin is replenished by the oils, you will encounter sensations in areas that are worked too hard on a daily basis, such as the neck, shoulders, and feet.

Craniosacral massage is another specialty here. The benefits of craniosacral therapy may not be noticed right away, but as you return to your routine, you will find the strength and energy to carry you through. The treatment is a very spiritual session involving the nervous system. Craniosacral work can help to alleviate stress issues, acute and chronic pain, and mental disturbances, and can help develop well-being and good health. The therapist is highly skilled at working the layer between the skull and the brain.

Before or after your treatment, relax in one of the four in-ground hot pools by the lake. Although these are not natural hot springs, they are wonderful for the muscles. There are teepees located near the pools where you can change, and towels can be found everywhere. Finally, don't forget to enjoy lunch in the grand dining hall while capturing the magnificent view through the large windows. This spa escape is truly one worth taking.

- Featured treatments: Raindrop Therapy, Craniosacral Massage
- 10% discount
- Hours: Daily 9:00 AM–7:00 PM (Closed Monday through Wednesday from January to April)

Body & Sole Day Spa

9140 Wadsworth Blvd. • Westminster, CO 80003

303-423-0102 • www.bodyandsolespa.com

Are you looking for a spa that can do it all?
Body & Sole Day Spa can.

At the corner of Wadsworth and 92nd, you will find a Tuscan village where vines climb the walls and friends gather to celebrate life. The Tuscan style extends to each room inside the spa, and they all have their own Italian name. Waterfalls add to the setting, and you will even find mints on your massage table to enjoy before your service. Welcome to Body & Sole, where the therapists can take care of you from head to toe.

Owner Debbie Rumble has quite a business. At Body & Sole, you can expect a cozy and friendly spa experience with comprehensive offerings. The 5,000-square-foot spa, which has been open for five years, has 60 employees, so whatever you want to have done is likely possible. Body & Sole is very supportive of its customers—not only do they offer a full-service salon with a separate reception area and its own music, but they provide tips, daily and monthly specials, and newsletters, all aimed at living a healthy lifestyle. They even have spa characters, The Sole Sisters, who provide light entertainment and education for regulars via e-mail.

From the Vichy shower and hydrotherapy tub to facials, manicures, and pedicures, all your desires for self-care are housed here. The spa is open seven days a week and has great night, weekend, and holiday hours. Both the men's and women's locker rooms provide steams and showers. There is a social pedicure area and a circular relaxing room with big chairs and a fireplace. Body & Sole is a spectacular location for parties; groups of 10 or more will receive a discount on their services.

As you might expect, the product area here is more like its own store. There are numerous things to choose from, including Crocs, bags, makeup, skin-care products, and more. The abundant offerings include brands such as Dermalogica, SkinCeuticals, Thymes, and Colorescience.

The name Body & Sole says it all: feet are a specialty. Treat yourself to the IonCleanse-and-reflexology combo. This 70-minute service is sure to leave you feeling better for months. Each day toxins are trapped in our tissues. The IonCleanse is aimed at releasing those toxins through the feet. It is an easy and pain-free experience—just sit back and watch how the toxins released from your system change the color of the water. Next, you will be escorted to the reflexology chair and your therapist will go to work. There are only a few spas that offer authentic reflexology treatments, which is a technique of applying pressure to the feet and hands. Each point is connected to an organ or area in your body. Through this service, you can begin a healing and revitalizing process from the feet up. You must experience the relief this provides.

Body & Sole is a place you could take your daughter, grandmother, best friend, or husband for a great day away from reality. If you live in the Arvada, Westminster, or Broomfield areas, there is no reason to drive any farther for the perfect spa escape.

- Featured treatments: IonCleanse, Reflexology
- 10% discount
- Hours: Mon. 11:00 AM–4:00 PM,
  Tues.–Thur. 9:00 AM–8:00 PM,
  Fri. 9:00 AM–6:00 PM, Sat. 8:00 AM–5:00 PM,
  Sun. 12:00 PM–5:00 PM

A New Spirit
Wellness Center & Spa

4907 W. 29th Ave. • Denver, CO 80212

303-477-1652 • www.anewspirit.com

$

Float your worries away at A New Spirit.

Located in a historic neighborhood in the Denver Highlands with great restaurants nearby, A New Spirit features the only floatation tanks in Colorado. This 3,200-square-foot spa has six treatment rooms and two floatation rooms and is big in experience. The spa features a variety of body treatments and wraps, facials, and massages done by very skilled therapists. Sanitas is the featured skin-care product line. The treatments and customer service here are exceptional. The atmosphere is very comfortable, and you will feel at home.

Begin your experience with the ionic footbath, which detoxifies your organs, blood, lymph nodes, and cells. This treatment requires a reservation due to its high demand.

Next, give floatation a try. But what exactly is floatation? Owner Andrea Leigh describes it as a way to find the Zen moment. In particular, it is the moment when you have reached mental release. Are you wondering if floatation is a séancelike or levitation procedure? Don't worry, it is nothing like that—except that some clients say the experience is magical.

The floatation tank is filled with 10 inches of water that is set at body temperature and contains Epsom salts. The high content of salt allows for little use of chemicals to sanitize the tank, but the tanks are filtered between each client, and Leigh uses many natural enzymes to help keep them clean. While the tank looks similar to a space shuttle, it is very roomy and private. You may keep the door to the tank open or closed, depending on your preference. There is subtle light and soft music playing inside the tank. There is also a neck pillow, earplugs, and a call button within reach for your convenience. The tank is very safe, and the environment is conducive to allowing you to let go of all of your worries.

There is definitely a mind-over-matter thinking plane that goes along with floatation. On average, it takes most people three to five visits to truly let go and find the experience enlightening. But flotation is different for everyone. For example, when it seems like you are thinking or worrying too much, you may feel as though you are bumping into the walls of the tank. But when you set your intentions on letting go of your schedule and simply focus on your breathing, you can feel a sense of calm. Everyone should try this unique experience.

Before or after floating, treat yourself to a one-hour massage. The massage incorporates just the right pressure combined with stretching to make your body no longer feel compressed. Add an enhancement such as hot stones or craniosacral therapy to your massage to make it extra special.

The aura of this spa conveys Leigh's mission quite clearly: to promote wellness and a healthy life. So, as Leigh recommends, live an informed and healthy life, and visit A New Spirit.

- Featured treatment: Floatation
- 10% discount
- Hours: Mon. & Tues. 10:00 AM–8:00 PM,
  Thurs. & Sun. 11:00 AM–6:00 PM,
  Fri. & Sat. 9:00 AM–6:00 PM

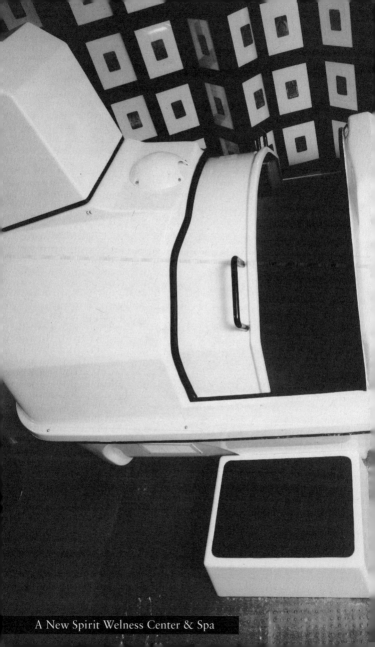

A New Spirit Welness Center & Spa

Oxford Club Spa, Salon, and Fitness Center

1616 17th St. • Denver, CO 80202

303-628-5435 • www.oxfordclubspa.com

*Are you looking for an unexpected
haven just off the downtown streets?
Make your way to the Oxford.*

Located in a historic building in the heart of LoDo, the Oxford provides clients with an extensive fitness center, salon, and spa, with overnight accommodations available right next door. With all of this, it might be hard for others to compete! Each of these aspects has its own dedicated section of the building, so although classes might be occurring in the fitness center and the salon could be filled with chatter, you would never know it inside the spa.

When you first enter the reception area, you will notice that the spa and salon is very open. You can see two stories of light pouring in. Fitness and spa products line the walls.

Walking along the red carpet and up the stairs, you make your way toward relaxation.

There are nine treatment rooms within this 14,000-square-foot building, each of which contains antique furniture that was originally brought over from Europe for the hotel. Wandering from room to room, you can see that these antiques have their own charm and style. There is also a secluded pedicure room upstairs that is spacious enough to enjoy with a group of friends.

At the Oxford, the difference is in the details. The spa aims to exceed guests' expectations by surprising them with little extras added to every service. Manager Heather Johnson's 12 years of spa-industry experience are evident in the integration of these details and the phenomenal products used in the services. The Oxford has so many signature touches in their offerings it will be hard for you to choose what you would like to have done. But overall, all of the treatments are aimed at helping you on a deep and powerful level.

There is a high standard of education among employees and amazing longevity—most have been with the Oxford an average of 10 years! Customer feedback is continually used to help them improve their service. Each new client is provided with a gift certificate for a discounted service in the future in exchange for his or her comments.

The spa offers a combination of organic and traditional services. One product line that is said to step it up a notch is Dr. Hauschka's.

These products are biodynamically grown, and every part of the plant is used so nothing goes to waste. Ask for the Dr. Hauschka Classic Facial Treatment.

The Thai Massage is offered in either an 80-minute or 105-minute session. It is unique in that the massage is done while you are fully clothed; a traditional Thai outfit is provided for you to wear. Plan to rock away your deep muscle tension while you experience acupressure and the relief of deep stretching.

The signature Moor Mud Wrap lasts for 105 minutes. Moor mud is made of natural peat material that is rich in protein, trace minerals, and vitamins, and helps ease aches and pains of the muscles and joints. This exfoliating service begins with a body brushing that is then followed by a relaxing moor mud soak. While you are soaking, you will be treated to a soothing cool-stone face massage. Your treatment will be completed with your own customized massage using moor body lotion.

Although the Oxford is both a day spa and a destination spa, and visitors of the adjoining hotel do frequent the spa, the majority of the clientele is local. With its fitness center open seven days a week and several salon stylists on hand, the Oxford is a home for many locals and part of their daily routine. Gym members receive a bonus of 10 percent off salon and spa products and services.

- Featured treatments: Thai Massage, Moor Mud Wrap
- 10% discount
- Hours: Mon.–Fri. 9:00 AM–8:00 PM, Sat. 9:00 AM–6:00 PM, Sun. 9:00 AM–5:00 PM

The Spa at the Brown Palace Hotel

321 17th St. • Denver, CO 80202

303-312-8940 • www.brownpalacespa.com

Do you desire luxury downtown?
The Spa at the Brown Palace is
where you will find it.

The Brown Palace has been a part of Denver history for over a hundred years. Its past is rich with the stories of people who have passed through its doors. Locals will likely tell you that their grandparents went on dates at the Brown. The ambiance here is unparalleled.

A new addition to the Brown Palace's offerings is its spa. Created with luxurious care for both men and women in mind, this spa captures what you would envision a day of lavishness to be. There are 20 therapists to cater to your every whim, including 12 massage therapists, 5 aestheticians, and 3 full-time nail technicians. In addition, the chef from Ellington's has created an organic spa cuisine that is designed to tempt all of your senses and complement the services you receive.

This downtown oasis takes you away the moment you walk into its magnificent lobby. It is

Victorian in decor, but infused with touches of Wild West charm. The spa boutique is filled with products such as Eminence and Phytomer. You can even take home trial-size samples to see if you like the products. You won't be disappointed!

The 5,000-square-foot spa spans two floors, one on the lobby level of the hotel and one below. There is a parlor for your hair, nail, and makeup care. The ladies' and gentlemen's areas each include showers, steam rooms, and lounges. Baskets of food, tea, coffee, and water are provided in each. In the gentlemen's lounge, guests can enjoy watching a flat-screen television. If the spa were made up of these areas alone, it would be worth the splurge.

The couple's room is magnificent. A red curtain masks the beauty when you first enter, making it seem as though a grand theatrical performance is about to begin. Then the beauty is revealed: a tiled room with an immense 20-jet tub strewn with rose petals and an intricate chandelier hanging from above. For special occasions, you can have bottles of wine, chocolate-dipped strawberries, and roses delivered to this romantic room.

Another amazing aspect of this spa is its 750-foot artesian well. For decades, this well has delivered pure water to Brown Palace Hotel guests, and now you can enjoy this water in your treatments. You will likely want to try the Artesian Plunge, which is a jetted soak that can be enjoyed alone or with another.

The Brown Palace Signature Facial utilizes encapsulated oxygen treatments to purify the skin to allow it to breathe more easily. It is an extended facial that includes massage for a healthy glow. It is completed with a paraffin hand dip, hand massage, and peppermint foot rub.

The Signature Massage at the Brown Palace is a customized treatment that utilizes deep-tissue, reflexology, and Swedish techniques. It is a one-of-a-kind combination that will leave you feeling like you never have before.

Assistant director Paul Maliska explained that the mission of the Spa at the Brown Palace Hotel is to provide luxury services to all guests. He hopes that their experience will be one they talk about. You can be sure that your needs will be met here.

- Featured treatments: Signature Massage, Signature Facial, Artesian Plunge
- Hours: Mon.–Sat. 9:00 AM–9:00 PM, Sun. 9:00 AM–6:00 PM

The Woodhouse Day Spa

941 E. 17th Ave. • Denver, CO 80218

303-813-8488 • www.denver.woodhousespas.com

*Are you looking for award-winning decor
and services? Visit The Woodhouse Day Spa.*

The Merritt House, built in 1889, is the home
of The Woodhouse Day Spa. An elegant
historic mansion, it is quite impressive from the
outside. The interior has been lovingly renovated
with the period of the building in mind. You
will come here not only for a treatment, but to
admire the entire building and its decor, which
enhance the inviting ambiance. Each room has
its own motif, but the Victorian theme is carried
throughout. Black-and-white photographs of Denver grace the walls and remind you that you are
in the middle of the city, which is easy to forget
when you are inside such a peaceful enclave.

Owner Tina Lovelace-Sporkin described the
mission of The Woodhouse as to "making people
feel like they are coming home." She and her husband, Jeff, have created something that is argu-
ably better than home.

Many special areas at this spa await your
arrival. Your complimentary glass of wine or tea

can be enjoyed while waiting in the sitting room prior to your services. The sunporch that wraps around the house is an exceptional area for lunch or just visiting.

Patrons will not be disappointed when visiting The Woodhouse, touted as the best day spa chain in America. The spa caters to locals and out-of-town guests. There are separate men's and women's lounge areas, and one of the 10 treatment rooms is perfect for couples. The spa is not pretentious, but still includes all the elements that make a spa great, including attention to detail, attentive therapists, and customized care. You will feel well taken care of here, as the employees are very experienced and fill the air with their positive energy.

The Woodhouse Day Spa has a catalog full of treatments, as there are so many offerings. Packages, body wraps, facials, massages, and more are available. Rare East-meets-West therapies such as the Shirodhara Scalp Massage, a healing technique from India that combines essential oils with a scalp massage, are also available. And The Woodhouse has the most immense pedicure room we have ever seen, making it ideal for parties or corporate events. There is also a well-organized product and gift area; gifts can be tailored to the requests of guests.

The Detoxifying Seaweed Wrap, a favorite at The Woodhouse, is a wonderful 75 minutes long. This service begins with a dry body brush followed by an application of essential oils. A seaweed paste is then used to nourish your body. Next, you can expect a scalp massage and a Vichy shower that vacillates between 90°F and 60°F every 45 seconds. You will leave feeling unimaginably refreshed.

It is not surprising that The Woodhouse has received many awards for its impressive atmosphere and treatments. The Denver location is even rated as the best Woodhouse in the country!

- Featured treatment: Detoxifying Seaweed Wrap
- 10% discount
- Hours: Daily 9:00 AM–7:00 PM

Rain Spa Bodyworks

310 St. Paul St. • Denver, CO 80206

303-388-2408 • www.rainspabodyworks.com

$

*Looking to escape for an hour or two? Visit
Rain Spa Bodyworks in Cherry Creek.*

Rain Spa is not your average frilly day spa;
rather, it is a spa that takes massage seri-
ously. Owner Nancy DuPont feels that positive
touch is one of the most precious gifts we can
give. Her philosophy is to be as holistic and natural as possible.

Purposeful intention is behind everything at
Rain Spa. An eclectic mix of symbolic artifacts
from Africa, South America, Egypt, and Indone-
sia comprises the decor. The colors on the walls
and the paintings on display are symbolic as well.
The colors represent the essence of Colorado,
with hues of rich forest green, balancing gold, and
tranquil terra-cotta. Da Vinci's drawing *Vitruvian
Man*, represents the movement of the body.

This 2,000-square-foot spa has five treatment
rooms with two additional rooms for nails. The
therapists have more than 31 years of combined

experience to draw from. Each therapist has his or her own unique style. For example, DuPont enjoys using noninvasive techniques along with mixing in thermal therapy (heat and water). In fact, Rain Spa was named for DuPont's love of aquatic treatments and the sweet air that is reminiscent of a cool rain. Other therapists enjoy using deep-tissue modality and integrating myofascial techniques.

Rain Spa offers a variety of treatments and products from around the globe. Massage treatments are most often requested, but spa packages are reasonably priced so that you can make the most of your day. The facials here are tailored to your specific needs for calming, firming, or detoxifying. The wraps are intended to relax, revitalize, reduce aches, rehydrate, and cleanse. Try the Dead Sea Mud Treatment to detoxify and restore a general balance to your system. This service integrates 400 medicinal herbs within the mud. Next, to experience the true sensation of the fundamental elements of a spa, immerse yourself in the Vichy shower, which combines steam and water. Or take advantage of a massage-and-pedicure combination. Like the facials, the massages are tailored to your individual needs and can be either deep, Swedish, or in between. The effects of the massage will diffuse overworked muscles and leave your body feeling elongated. Afterward, enjoy a pedicure that includes soaking and exfoliating your feet while you are seated on a vibrating massage chair.

The therapists at Rain Spa are very flexible and can accommodate small parties with various treatments. Whether you are looking for a spiritual vibration or decompressing, the therapists at Rain Spa Bodyworks are educated and able to honor your request.

- Featured treatments: Massages, Pedicures
- Added-value promotions
- Hours: Tues.–Sat. 10:00 AM–6:00 PM, Sun. & Mon. appointments upon request

Antoine du Chez
The Spa at Cherry Creek

150 Clayton Ln. • Denver, CO 80206

303-320-6012 • www.antoineduchez.com

*Pamper yourself from head to toe
and bask in the delight of Cherry Creek's
offerings at Antoine du Chez.*

Our time at Antoine du Chez: The Spa at Cherry Creek was not just an afternoon spent at the salon, but a spa phenomenon. Hospitality and quality make this experience what a day spa should strive to be. Here, visitors feel like they are not only being pampered, but lavishly spoiled. Antoine du Chez is well worth the convenient drive from any Denver suburb.

The spa resides in the JW Marriott in Cherry Creek North. The 11-floor, 191-room hotel is ranked by *Condé Nast Traveler* as one of the top 100 hotels in the United States. Located only two blocks from the Cherry Creek Shopping Center, the spa and salon emphasize the physiology of touch while maintaining a respectful intimacy that leaves the client with a positive feeling. The expertise found here is a reflection of the immense knowledge that spa president Robert Miller has to offer from his 32 years in the industry. Antoine du Chez is a leader in the hair fashion and aesthetics industries and has its own training facility in Denver. There are two other locations within the metro Denver region, although we only visited The Spa at Cherry Creek.

The spa and salon cater to men and women. The location, ambience, and services add up to an event you will not want to miss. At Antoine du Chez, a calming retreat to rid chaos from your busy life awaits you. Upon entering the spa, subdued lighting helps create an environment for relaxation. The locker rooms provide ample space in which to prepare yourself to enjoy the next few hours. Outside the locker room, you will find a centrally located fireplace where you can soak your feet, perhaps enjoy a glass of wine, and talk among friends before your services.

Along with massages, facials, and body treatments, this spa offers many nail- and hair-care treatments. These are done in a separate area filled with natural light pouring through big windows, which also treat you to a view of Cherry Creek North. There is a private dining area for guests to enjoy food and beverages while relaxing in their robes. Antoine du Chez feature the Ling skin-care line, and they carry Kérastase, J Beverly Hills, and American Crew hair products.

The Hot-Stone Massage integrates the philosophy of a feng shui cleanse. Negative energy is released from the tapping of a rock onto another rock at specific pressure points on the body. The discharge of endorphins in the brain allows for an emotional release that creates a wave upon which your tensions will ride away. The thing to remember is that the heat should not be felt immediately; instead, you should feel a slow easing process that enables you to breathe and let go.

The Reflexology Treatment is spellbinding in the palms of therapist Gerlinde Hackney. You might even fall asleep! She possesses excellent knowledge and awareness of this therapy, which is imperative for finding where the troubled spots are. Many spas offer reflexology or foot treatments, but in order to reap the most benefits for your body, it is important to check whether the therapists are trained in reflexology, as Hackney is.

There is no rush to conclude your experience here. A complimentary blow-dry and style will make you feel ready to take on the town again, or just feel good about yourself as you dissolve into your own relaxed state for the evening. Your makeup can be done as well.

Stay at Antoine du Chez for an hour, a day, or the whole weekend for pampering—you will be glad you did. This is an ideal place to make time stop, or at least slow down.

- Featured treatments: Hot-Stone Massage, Reflexology Treatment
- 15% discount
- Hours: Mon. 9:00 AM–7:00 PM,
  Tues.–Thurs. 9:00 AM–8:00 PM,
  Fri. 8:30 AM–7:30 PM,
  Sat. 8:00 AM–7:00 PM, Sun. 9:00 AM–5:00 PM
  (Closed on major holidays)

The Wax House

9552 E. 27th Ave. • Denver, Colorado 80238

303-523-3782 • www.waxhouse.net

$$

*If you are looking for a spa that offers
natural skin care in a place children are
always welcome, you will not be disap-
pointed with The Wax House.*

In the heart of the newly revived Stapleton area,
The Wax House provides an inviting way for
you to take care of yourself. You will be pleas-
antly surprised that you stumbled onto this find,
tucked away in a small residential neighborhood.
If you live close by, you can even find your way
there on foot, as many of the regulars do. Though
small, what this little spa lacks in size it makes up
in high-quality treatments, decor, and unparal-
leled personalized service.

Upon arrival, you are welcome to peruse
the natural products that are artistically arranged
on glass shelves and available for purchase. The
atmosphere here can be described as both com-
fortable and chic. The Wax House is the result
of an evolution for owner and aesthetician

Tawyna Hutchinson, who used to own a large spa in Denver. Now focused on a simple, natural way of living, she provides excellent service at a great price in her local spa. Look for frequently discounted rates on skin-care products and service packages.

As you enter The Wax House, it is evident that skin care is the specialty here, and it is done very well—the skin of the customers leaving the spa is literally glowing, allowing their natural beauty to shine through. It makes you think that they know a secret or two. Therapists approach skin-care improvement by getting to know the client's needs, then teaching the client how to take care of his or her skin through a regime of natural products and regular exfoliation. Men, women, and teens frequent The Wax House to maintain their skin and partake in relaxation.

Along with featuring a specialized technique for nearly pain-free waxing, The Wax House offers several facials, including the House Facial, the Teen Facial, the Gentleman's Facial, the Mini Facial, and the Peel. There are also many add-on services, such as the Hot-Oil Scalp Treatment and the Eye Treatment.

The Hot-Oil Scalp Treatment allows you to have a scalp massage as a part of any service. Hot aromatic oils are used for hydration, and a luxurious towel wrap infuses moisture into the hair. When you return home, make sure to shampoo your hair *before* getting it wet in the shower so it can by styled easily and does not remain too oily.

The House Facial is a completely customized service. It is one of the treatments The Wax House is known for. Your face will be pampered and transformed through face, neck, and décolletage care. Heated hand mitts and a green-tea eye compress add to this indulgence, which can be either 60 or 90 minutes in length. It is absolute perfection.

A particularly unique feature of this spa is that it is tailored toward the busy mom—your little ones have their own play space right within your treatment room.

- Featured treatments: House Facial, Hot-Oil Scalp Treatment, Waxing
- 30% discount
- Hours: Tues.–Thurs. 12:00 PM–8:00 PM, Wed., Fri., & Sat. 9:00 AM–4:00 PM

South Denver

Izba Spa
Russian Body Therapy

17908 B Cottonwood Dr. • Parker, CO 80134

303-400-1001 • www.izbaspa.com

1441 York St. • Denver, CO 80206

303-321-1239 • www.izbaspa.com

$

Sore muscles? Stressed?
Just want to leave it all behind?

Welcome to Izba Spa: Russian Body Therapy. Izba, translated as "a cozy log cabin," has two locations for you to sample. The original is in downtown Denver, and the newest addition is in Parker.

Leo LeVyssokov is the owner of Izba in Denver. He has provided Banya therapy to members of the Colorado Ballet, renowned figure skaters, and even the Colorado Avalanche. An Izba therapist actually travels with the team, and between seasons the team frequents the spa. Karen Chesser is the owner of the Parker location, found in a quiet strip mall and decorated in a Russian fantasy theme. You will not believe how you will be transported to a new realm of restoration while experiencing Izba's prized services.

The healing effects of Russian Banya therapy have been around for centuries. Following WWI, the therapy became widespread throughout the rest of the world when it was incorporated with medical science due to a shortage of supplies. Banya therapy's reliance on natural practices and materials, including massage, herbs, and heat, came into play to heal patients. Banya is as commonly used in Russia as jogging is in America for maintaining good health.

It is a spectacular practice to help reduce stress and relax. The treatment uses a wet sauna in combination with massage performed with honey and then a brisk brushing of oak leaves. This increases body temperature, stimulates circulation, and strengthens the immune system. The therapy is then followed by a cooldown. The experience is highly detoxifying; however, please note that this treatment may not be comfortable at first for those who are modest.

The Banya room is heated to between 175° and 180°F. It can be regulated by the therapist and ventilated, if you wish. Water is poured over rocks to heat the room, followed by essential oil. Next, the sweating begins. The therapist applies honey and oils to the body. Oak leaves, taken from Colorado's mountains, are then heated on the rocks. When the leaves are warmed, the therapist rustles them in the air, making more heat and steam. Then the therapist uses the leaf broom to pat your body. The heat is very regulated to complete the Banya treatment correctly. A cool shower follows. However, the experience is not over yet—you then have a massage, followed by another Banya, and then your final shower. The massage is grand and includes a stomach massage, which is very soothing and great for digestion and detoxification. Your stomach is an important energy center. When it is massaged, it can be revitalized.

You will be well taken care of as your therapist leads you through this treatment, so go ahead and try something new. You will leave with your worries, stress, toxins, and troubles all behind, and will not feel denied at The Izba Spa.

- Featured treatments: Banya therapy and massage
- 10% discount
- Hours: Mon.–Sat. 9:00 AM–9:00 PM, Sun. 9:00 AM–7:00 PM

The Spa at the Inverness

200 Inverness Dr. West • Englewood, CO 80112

800-832-9053 • www.invernesshotel.com

*Seeking a comfortable, classy spa getaway
that offers a top-notch hotel, food, and
pool? Look no further than the Inverness.*

Just off of C-470 and I-25 in the Denver Tech Center is a year-old addition to the Denver-area spa offerings. And what an addition it is! Whether you prefer the top echelon of spas or the small local kind, you will not be disappointed here, as The Spa at the Inverness comprises the best of both worlds. The atmosphere is refined and authentic. It is a combination that allows both the first-time spa-goer and the spa connoisseur to be satisfied simultaneously. The final project of a $9 million renovation at the Inverness, this spa continues to gather quite a buzz around town.

The entry to the spa is completely separate from the hotel's. Even as you take your first step inside, you know that you made a great choice. No detail has been ignored. The warm, rich colors, ambient light, and decor combine to welcome you to a unique urban experience. Take a moment to peruse the products for sale, then walk over the gorgeous tile to the full-size men's or women's locker room. Each is complete with granite countertops, showers, a eucalyptus steam room, and every amenity imaginable, including lotions, curling irons, brushes, and more.

When you are ready, the curved walls guide you as you make your way to one of the seven treatment rooms, which are elegant and comfortable and just the right size for a personal retreat. You will easily be able to unwind and relax in your surroundings. One room contains an amazing Swiss shower with 12 heads. There is also a pedicure room with a bench seat and Sanijet tubs that ensure cleanliness. A pre- and post-relaxation suite, where you can be served lunch, have tea, and read, overlooks a private outdoor area that features a hot tub and fireplace. As a spa guest, you also have access to the pool and fitness center. And don't miss out on the incredible couple's room, which is complete with custom tile and a quiet, pipeless soaking tub.

The mission of The Spa at the Inverness is to give each guest an individual journey to relaxation. The therapists are genuinely friendly and kind, and strive to bring you the best. From the reception you receive at the front desk to the service you experience during your treatment, you will feel like you are the only one at the spa. Whether you desire a full day of pampering or a break in the middle of your day, the therapists will give you time that is meant just for you. Team members are trained to individualize each spa treatment so everyone has a unique experience and no one treatment will ever be exactly the same. You can even bring in your own iPod to customize your musical selection. The therapists know that downtime is rare, and they feel that everyone has different needs and deserves to have those needs met.

You will not want to miss the divine 80-minute Devote and Detox. The body is purified with a Moroccan mint tea silt, followed by a lemon–coffee blossom scrub, then moisturized with a tangerine-fig butter crème that illuminates your body and revives your soul.

The 50-minute Hydrating Facial is based on the idea that the key to beautiful skin is hydration. This innovative facial is ideal for dry, water-starved skin. Your skin will be bathed in Phytomer's patented ingredient Pheohydrane, a brown seaweed extract that significantly improves the skin's ability to be a more effective water-binding mechanism. It will leave your skin feeling immediately hydrated and will result in your complexion feeling smooth and looking radiant.

Join the customers of The Spa at the Inverness who describe it as a total escape.

- Featured treatments: Devote and Detox, Hydrating Facial
- Complimentary aromatherapy upgrade with any massage
- Hours: Mon.–Sat. 9:00 AM–8:00 PM, Sun. 9:00 AM–6:00 PM

Spavia Day Spa

8283 S. Akron St., Ste. 150 • Centennial, CO 80112

303-858-1234 • www.spaviadayspa.com

Looking for a way to maintain your well-being monthly? Spavia, interpreted as "wellness," could be your answer.

Spavia may be small, but it is very large in concept, as the mission of this spa is to provide monthly maintenance and wellness at an affordable price. The concept of a membership-based spa is revolutionizing the spa industry. At Spavia, for $49 a month you can receive a massage or facial and additional discounts for any other services during that month. Although there are other spas that offer memberships, unlike the majority of those, Spavia does not present a clinical type of environment. Another nice thing about this spa is that there is no long-term commitment on your membership, and they offer varying levels of programs. For example, the Signature level is for healthy skin, the Premier level is for antiaging services and is geared toward active, all-natural treatments, and the Ultimate level includes longer combination treatments. The benefits of a membership also include a rewards program.

Owner Allyson Langenderser is very particular about the therapists she hires and the environment that is created within the walls of the spa. You will not find tacky magazines here; rather, there is an offering of self-improvement resources for your reading pleasure. And Langenderser promotes local artists and musicians by displaying their artwork and playing their music softly. Due to the location—which is in a very busy strip mall—sound soothers are used to keep the treatment rooms quiet. Subtle lighting also plays a critical role in creating a calming effect in each retreat room.

Langenderser is particular about Spavia's impact on the environment. Her collection of products includes pure mineral makeup and parabens- and preservative-free ingredients.

The menu of services offered here for both men and women is extensive. The therapists at Spavia really work toward customizing treatments to every individual. The Signature Facial includes a skin analysis along with cleansing, aromatic steaming, an enzyme mask, and rehydration. Afterward, your skin will feel soft and refreshed. During this treatment, you will find yourself relaxing while the therapist massages your neck, shoulders, arms, and hands.

If it is a body treatment you are looking for, look no further. Spavia offers a wide array of services to revitalize your skin. The Deep Hydrating

Wrap begins with exfoliating dead skin cells. The body scrub includes a mixture of shea and cocoa butters and honey. Your head, neck, and shoulders will be massaged as you are wrapped in lavender body butter. The Vitamin E in the body butter will help regenerate your skin, making it feel soft and healthy once more.

Although Spavia may appear small, don't let the size fool you, as there are separate retreat rooms for men and women to rest in. In addition, there is a sliding door that opens up for larger, festive gatherings. In fact, Langenderser has conjured the term *spa-lebration* to convey "wellness and celebration." Take advantage of your membership benefits and bring a special person in with you at a discount so that you can enjoy the day together.

- Featured treatment: Signature Facial
- $20.00 off Signature Massage or Signature Facial
- Hours: Mon.–Fri. 10:00 AM–8:00 PM,
  Sat. 9:00 AM–6:00 PM, Sun. 11:00 AM–6:00 PM

Coldwater Creek
The Spa

329 S. Teller St. • Lakewood, CO 80226

303-975-8736 • www.coldwatercreekthespa.com

$$ ❮❙❯

*With your shopping bag in hand, get ready
to spend an enjoyable afternoon with your
girlfriends or just some well-deserved time
alone at Coldwater Creek: The Spa.*

Take advantage of Coldwater Creek spa.
One of only seven nationwide, this one is in
our very own backyard. Located in the shopping
village of Belmar, Coldwater Creek: The Spa pro-
vides you with an urban experience. While the spa
is part of a corporation, the services received here
are very personalized. Coldwater Creek stores,
specializing in women's clothing, opened their
doors in 1984 and have been recognized as num-
ber-one in customer service for specialty apparel
retailers. The standards they strive for as clothiers
are no less apparent at the spa, as each and every
therapist is required to undergo extensive training.

This spa, which is located behind the store-
front, is like being at a friend's house where you

instantly feel relaxed because she has taken care of all the details without overwhelming the senses. The colors used here are serene and simple. Upon entering, leave your busy life outside, and change into comfy robes and sandals. The locker rooms are spacious, and every amenity is provided, from shower necessities to finishing hair products. Seated in the relaxation room, you are treated to a eucalyptus foot soak, and the tension in your neck begins to subside from the warm, clove-filled neck pillow that is provided. Add a cup of freshly bagged tea and the relaxation stage is well under way. The massage and facial beds are comfortable, automatically heated, and adjustable. The down covers invite a well-deserved snooze.

The Vitamin C Facial includes a luxurious massage for the face, neck, and shoulder area. This special antiaging facial cleanses, purifies, and moisturizes. It combines the elements of aromatherapy, acupressure, exfoliation, and massage. It even incorporates hydrating hand therapy. You will feel pampered as your skin rejuvenates during this process. You will leave with some vitamin C serum in hand to revitalize your cells, as well as tips on how to better care for your skin at home.

The Ultimate Pedicure is a Coldwater Creek exclusive. After you choose your nail color, recline in the zero-gravity chair, where you will begin your journey into deep relaxation. A heated neck cushion, a soft warm blanket, and a lavender-filled eye pillow are lovely invitations to dreamland. During the aromatherapy, you will be asked to inhale and exhale essential oils as you enter a transcendent state of relaxation. You will have an exquisite experience when the therapist performs an extensive massage that concentrates on specific acupressure points from your knees to your toes. The Ultimate Pedicure combines so many wonderful aspects of exfoliation and massage into the same service that by the time you are done, you will be wondering what treatment you came in for.

The spa offers a wonderful selection of lotions and potions and comfortable spa clothing. Visiting Coldwater Creek: The Spa left us with a renewed and reenergized feeling that made us ready to restart the day. Come to celebrate a special occasion or take advantage of a spa package and indulge yourself. In the words of a Coldwater Creek representative, "Your mind and body will be taken away. No travel necessary."

- Featured treatments: Ultimate Pedicure, Vitamin C Facial
- Weekly specials
- Hours: Mon.–Sat. 9:00 AM–8:00 PM, Sun. 9:00 AM–5:00 PM

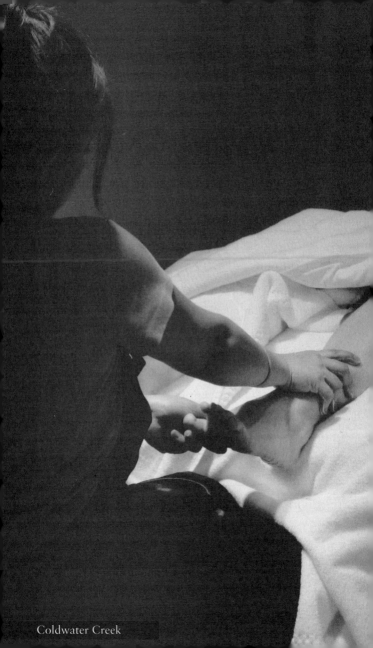
Coldwater Creek

Lavender Fields

108 Market St. • Morrison, CO 80465

303-697-1959 • www.lavenderfieldsbeautyretreat.com

*Want a unique spa with a quaint
mountain-town ambiance?
Lavender Fields is just the place for you.*

Set at the east entrance to Red Rocks in Morrison, Lavender Fields is a special retreat for anyone and everyone to enjoy. This little purple spa is truly a treasure. It is just out-of-the-way enough to restore perspective to your busy life, but conveniently located only minutes from C-470. Where else can you experience a day of restoration where the city brushes up against the mountains' edge?

The historic mansion that houses Lavender Fields was built in 1873, just a year before the 2.6-mile-long town of Morrison was officially formed. There is a charming small-town feel, with the local town hall just across the street. You can hear birds chirping and soothing water running as you approach the spa, so be sure to take the time to enjoy the fresh mountain air before your service.

Creative souls, this is your place. The spa is infused with lavender inside and out, and the mirrors and walls are adorned with words like *Loved* and *Embellish*. Each treatment room has its own theme. The couple's room is covered in sunflowers, and the aesthetician's room rests among the clouds. Men who visit are often quite in awe of it all, and women usually describe feeling like they are at a comfortable, homey getaway.

Owner Joette Vanderhoven's welcoming and genuine demeanor permeates the entire spa. It is clear that this is where she wants to be. Her 27 years of experience ensure excellent service for all who visit.

This amazing little place boasts quite an impressive variety of services, including craniosacral, reflexology, and trigger-point massage. Trigger-point massage and reflexology share the goal of providing relief through the application of pressure, either directly to specific points in the body or through the feet. Craniosacral, or head, massage is a treatment aimed at improving your ability to focus. Couple's massages are also available, along with several other facial, massage, manicure, and pedicure choices. There is even a full-service hair salon that can help to ensure you look your best upon leaving. Treatments here can be personalized to the needs of the individual or group.

The River Stone Facial, River Stone Massage, and River Stone Pedicure are not to be missed. The massage can be either 60, 90, or 120 minutes long—can you imagine? The stones are hot and used throughout the treatment with the mission of the spa in mind, which is to "embrace the beauty within." This massage is especially beneficial if you would like deep penetration of your muscles without a lot of pressure. It is very relaxing. For a real escape, combine this service with the 90-minute signature River Stone Facial, which uses basalt rocks to continue the relaxation process.

The River Stone Pedicure begins with an extensive warm-stone foot and leg massage and a mineral mud pack to add moisture and remove toxins. Before the polish is applied, the feet are wrapped in warm towels for added pampering. It is very relaxing.

A day at Lavender Fields is reminiscent of an afternoon spent at your grandmother's home. This is a great venue for an intimate bridal shower or party. If four friends book three services each, the place is yours alone.

- Featured treatments: River Stone Facial, River Stone Massage, River Stone Pedicure
- 10% discount
- Hours: Tues.–Sat. 10:00 AM–5:00 PM, Sun. & Mon. by appointment only

Urban Escape Day Spa

700 12th St., #130 • Golden, CO 80401

303-278-1709 • www.urbanescapespa.com

*Find yourself escaping again and again
to revitalize your mind and body
in downtown Golden.*

Downtown Golden has long awaited a full day spa that offers a menu of services sure to please everyone. The name of the spa says it all: this is an urban escape. Opened in September 2007, this spa has already proven to be a golden gem (pun intended) that comes through on its promises. Not only does Urban Escape give back to the local community and sponsor many charities, but the staff here provides the most impeccable attention to their guests. The use of earth tones, candlelight, relaxing music, and mild fragrances create an intimate environment.

You will be amazed at how luxurious this spa feels. The treatment rooms are spacious, and the locker rooms are well equipped. The services at Urban Escape promote stress relief, balance, and wellness, and are tailored to each individual's needs. Choose from a variety of facials, pedicures, massages, and body treatments, as well as special packages.

Some of the specialty treatments include the Vitamin C Citrus Facial, the True Reveal Antiaging Peel Treatment with Idebenone, and the Ice Cream Pedicure. Vitamin C products helps reduce the appearance of sun damage and hyperpigmentation. The antiaging treatment is a chemical peel that will replenish your skin and make it appear youthful once again. The Ice Cream Pedicure includes a scoop-of-ice-cream foot fizz, a sherbet scrub, a chocolate or marshmallow foot mask, and foot icing to top it all off. Indulge in an ice cream social with your friends—it's sure to be a hit!

If you can spare three hours, escape with the Urban Getaway. This package includes a massage, facial, and pedicure—three different treatments, three different therapists, and each is wonderful. The facial begins with a "warm welcome," which includes warm towels placed under your neck, across your décolletage, and over your forehead. During the facial, your hands will be treated to a sugar scrub, hand cream, and warm mitts. This treatment is very thorough. Your skin will be cleansed, exfoliated, toned, and moisturized with Sanitas skin-care products that are just right for your skin type. Your face will then be massaged by the therapist's soothing hands, and your lips and eyes will not be ignored, as they, too, will be treated with moisturizers and serums. Feeling refreshed, your getaway will continue with a therapeutic massage that meets your specific needs. It includes stretching your limbs and applying the correct amount of pressure your body desires. After the massage, sit back (literally) and enjoy the final phase of this package as your feet are pampered for the next hour. Fall asleep, dream, let your worries seem far away. When you wake, your toes will shine, your feet will feel soft, and you will be ready to take on the day. But if you want to hold off on reentering reality quite yet, enjoy some peace in the relaxation room. You might find yourself never wanting to leave...

- Featured treatment: Urban Getaway
- 10% discount
- Hours: Tues., Wed., & Fri. 9:00 AM–7:00 PM, Thurs. 9:00 AM–8:00 PM, Sat. 9:00 AM–5:30 PM, Sun. 1:00 PM–5:00 PM

TallGrass
Aveda Spa & Salon

997 Upper Bear Creek Rd. • Evergreen, CO 80439

303-670-4444 • www.tallgrassspa.com

*Looking for a spa experience to take you
away from the hustle and bustle but not
too far away from Denver's city limits?
Pay a visit to TallGrass.*

Evergreen is an easy drive on I-70, just 45
minutes from downtown Denver. At 7,200
feet, it is a town known for its access to mountain
activities such as hiking, biking, and skiing, as
well as its cultural offerings. As you drive beyond
40-acre Evergreen Lake, you will find TallGrass
situated in a meadow surrounded by the mountains. The expansive views and fresh air will
engulf you, and nearby dense trees sweep the sky,
offering you a secluded location for a day of rest.
The lodge-style decor is both elegant and rustic, a
perfect complement to the rural location. You will
be graciously greeted, and then simply asked to
leave your shoes behind.

There are 11 different day packages, ranging

from 2-hour to 9-hour escapes. There are 9 types of facials, 9 different massages, and 12 body treatment offerings. Add the full-service hair salon and 10 nail-care choices, and it is easy to see why TallGrass is a favorite among visitors and residents of Colorado.

This spa is just the right size for a day spent with a friend or loved one. The pedicure room is designed so that you can sit side by side and enjoy each other's company. The treatment rooms are separate from this area and are extremely quiet.

TallGrass also has a private suite, The Sage Room, which contains a fireplace and a patio. This suite can be rented for an event such as a bridal shower or any other gathering. A catered meal can even be brought in for your enjoyment.

TallGrass caters to men and women. The Men's Tune-Up consists of a 50-minute thera-peutic massage, the Mountain Man Facial, and a haircut. The Mountain Man Facial is a deep-cleansing treatment that calms, soothes, and relieves irritated skin due to exposure from harsh, dry weather conditions. Tension is alleviated with a neck and shoulder massage.

The Caribbean Therapy Body Wrap is a wonderful rejuvenating treatment. This service uses massage with plant ingredients from the Caribbean to restore peace. It begins with a foot soak that exfoliates and masks your lower legs and feet. Next, a detoxifying seaweed mask is applied all over before you are wrapped in sheets and a blanket. You are then treated to a scalp and face massage. After a steam and shower, the therapist finishes with an application of lotion and one last massage.

Build in extra time to spend at TallGrass. Browse the Aveda products, music, clothing, and gifts on display, and take time to enjoy a lunch of fine spa cuisine while you relax and read on one of the three outdoor verandas.

- Featured treatment: Caribbean Therapy Body Wrap
- Hours: Mon.–Wed. 8:30 AM–7:30 PM, Thur. & Fri. 8:30 AM–6:30 PM, Sun. 10:00 AM–6:00 PM (Closed the first Monday of the month)

Whispering Pines
Massage & Day Spa

1262 Bergen Pkwy. • Bldg. E, #20 • Evergreen, CO 80439

303-674-7723 • www.whisperingpinesspa.com

Whispering Pines Massage & Day Spa
prides itself on providing a peaceful,
comfortable atmosphere.

A relaxing drive heading into Colorado's foot-hills will lead you to Whispering Pines. The spa is located in Evergreen, an upscale mountain community. Owners Marla Haley, Collette Kinkopf, and Lisa Wormer complement each other while creating a unique personality for their spa. Their display of professionalism is like that found in a bigger luxury spa, integrated into the charm of a quaint day spa.

The mountain-style decor and pine accents are warm and soothing. Behind the reception area, warm up by the cozy fireplace as you sit and relax while you wait before, after, or in between your treatments. Adjacent to the relaxation room is the nail station, where you and a friend can have a pedicure side by side. The restrooms are spacious, leaving ample room to change clothes and store your personal belongings in the provided lockers. A large steam shower is available to all spa guests. There are four treatment rooms tucked away in the back of the spa, where you can find some tranquility.

The services offered here support the athletic, outdoor lifestyles that make living in Colorado so enjoyable. Athletes who frequent the spa do so for maintenance, to deal with injuries, or to heal from their physically active and sports-minded lives. Other clients find themselves at Whispering Pines for a relaxing getaway. Massages are customized to meet individual needs. The spa can be also reserved for special occasions such as bridal showers, birthday parties, or even a ladies' night out.

The Hot-Stone Massage combines the fundamentals of deep-tissue work with the application of stones. The theory behind this treatment is that the stones absorb the natural elements from the sun and the environment, which the body then soaks up. A natural oil that helps the body absorb the heat from the stones is first massaged onto the skin. The therapist then applies pressure with a hot stone to the back, arms, and the backs of your legs. After finding the areas where the stress is held, the therapist aligns the stones vertically along your upper body. Stones are also placed beneath you so that you are lying on top of them. This may sound uncomfortable, but it is the furthest thing from it—you will find pure relaxation, and you might even fall asleep!

The Better-than-Botox Facial begins with a cleansing from milk and honey. A lactic-acid peel, to retexturize the skin, is given next. This is followed up by a Peptiderm antiaging serum, which improves lines and wrinkles, much like Botox does, but the advantage of this treatment is that no prescription is needed.

The people who work at the spa make you feel cared for. You will leave Whispering Pines feeling enlightened and recharged.

- Featured treatments: Hot-Stone Massage, Better-than-Botox Facial
- 10% discount
- Hours: Mon. 10:00 AM–5:00 PM, Tues.–Fri. 10:00 AM–7:00 PM, Sat. 10:00 AM–5:00 PM, Sun. 12:00 PM–5:00 PM

First Feather Day Spa

10601 CO Hwy. 73 • Conifer, CO 80433

303-838-2951 • www.firstfeather.com

*Take a day trip into the colorful foothills
to enjoy a local favorite.*

Vivian Martin, owner of First Feather Day Spa, in Conifer, has a strong belief in giving back to the community. The name of her spa was inspired by a Native American tradition of "teaching the young that members of a community must care for each other in order to succeed." Loyal customers of the spa find themselves catching up with neighbors or just enjoying the moment while sipping tea by the cozy fireplace.

First Feather offers rejuvenating body treatments. The therapists are innovative in the techniques and products they use. They incorporate Ayurvedic, Reiki, and other energy-work methods for deep relaxation, and together the staff has a tremendous number of years of experience in massage therapy and cosmetology. The spa features spa pedicures, a sauna, and a steam shower that is used with the body treatments.

The facials are designed around the Eminence line, which is created in Hungary and made from purely organic ingredients. With scents such as pomegranate and chocolate soufflé, you would think you could eat the facial rather than have it as a treatment. We highly suggest anything that features chocolate—yum! After all, when else can you feel guilt free when chocolate is involved? All of the scents in this product line are designed as active ingredients for specific purposes. For example, the cranberry-pomegranate is used for revitalizing all skin types, while the chocolate mousse hydrates normal to dry skin. After a treatment with Eminence, you will come out glowing, with your skin feeling refreshed and renewed.

First Feather offers a nice and easy way to help you build massage into your regular routine: you can purchase a series of massages ahead of time and schedule them when they best fit into your calendar. A benefit is that the price per massage works out to be a real savings. Also, purchasing a series of massages ensures that you are making a commitment to yourself.

The therapists at First Feather will take the time to assess your body for overworked areas prior to attacking those nasty knots. Whether it is with the use of stones or their hands, the staff ensures that the massages here will make you feel realigned and able to take on the world for another day.

We also recommend trying the new Ionic Foot Detox to detoxify your organs through your feet. You may want to do this on a regular basis.

This small-town spa offers great customer service, is always promoting monthly specials, and has a unique boutique.

- Featured treatment: Eminence Facial
- 10% discount plus a free skin-care analysis
- Hours: Please call

Colorado Wellness Spa

411 E. Bijou St. • Colorado Springs, CO 80903

719-598-3113 • www.cwdayspa.com

$$ 🍴

*Located near downtown Colorado Springs,
this 1891 Victorian house–turned-spa is a
perfect refuge for a celebration.*

Enjoy an hour, or two, or four—oh, go ahead, make a day out of it! You will be glad you did.

Natascha McCants, owner of Colorado Wellness, has finely blended a unique spa experience with elegant Victorian charm. The house is warm and comforting. The environment enables you to naturally slow down from your busy life. In fact, the ambience of this spa will delight all your senses. The peaceful sound of running water subtly fills the air. In the backyard, you will find a hot tub and outdoor sitting area. Inside the two-story house, there is a garden room toward the back where you can sit and relax or enjoy some lunch.

McCants takes pride in providing natural products that encourage health. Many of the treatments use products prepared from fresh ingredients, such as the milk-and-honey soaking bath and the strawberries-and-cream pedicure.

Begin your day by taking a dip in the hot tub prior to your services. If weather permits, as it so often does in Colorado, enjoy a gorgeous morning by unwinding outdoors while sipping on a special drink called a Cleanse Elixir, accompanied by fresh fruit. Your day might then continue with a 50-minute Sage Brush Massage, a lymphatic draining of the toxins stored in the body. A firm, positive touch will invigorate your body to a state of balance. Afterward, you will feel relaxed yet revitalized. The tension and stress can continue to melt away if you experience a mini Aromatherapy Scalp Treatment and an Ultimo Facial. Both your face and body will feel pampered. Think the day is done? Hold on, for if you choose, there is still more to come. Enjoy a Cucumber-and-Jasmine Soaking Bath in one of the antique Victorian tubs before finishing with a Grand Spa Pedicure. Throughout the day, you will indulge in mini cheesecakes, tea cookies, and chocolate-covered strawberries.

Colorado Wellness is a great place for escaping with a friend, spouse, or your mother or daughter. Here, you can spend quality time together reconnecting. Massages, facials, manicures, and pedicures can be done side by side, allowing more time to relax in each other's company.

Check out the website for the most recent offerings. This is a spa you will not want to miss.

Highlight it on the map for your next spa adventure, schedule it on the calendar, get in the car, and go!

- Featured treatments: Sage Brush Massage, Ultimo Facial, Soaks, Pedicures
- 10% discount
- Hours: Tues. & Wed. 9:00 AM–5:00 PM, Thurs. 9:00 AM–7:00 PM, Fri. & Sat. 8:00 AM–7:00 PM, Sun. & Mon. prebooked packages and groups by appointment only

Yevgeniya's Russian Day Spa

6977 N. Academy Blvd. • Colorado Springs, CO 80918

719-495-1049 • www.russiandayspa.com

$$

*Escape to the forest at
Yevgeniya's Russian Day Spa.*

You'll find Yevgeniya's via a pleasant drive through the charming countryside of the Black Forest, an unincorporated area in northeast Colorado Springs. This spa has grown from a small in-town locale to its own building in the forest. It is in a very secluded and relaxing location. To accompany its true foreign flair, the decor is internationally themed and includes the Russian Tea Room, European Room, and the Egyptian Room. There are seven different treatment rooms in all.

Yevgeniya means "noble and gracious." The name truly characterizes the personality of this spa. Owners Yevgeniya Chsheglova-Brazy and her husband, Chris Brazy, an entrepreneur, met in the Midwest. Chsheglova-Brazy is trained in physical therapy and as an internationally licensed Russian massage therapist and nurse practitioner. She chose not to work in the medical realm and decided that the spa business fit her goals. Her expertise has allowed her to create an extensive spa menu. Together, Chsheglova-Brazy and her husband have designed an oasis for healing and relaxation.

The mission at Yevgeniya's is to help people with ailments and discomfort and to enhance their busy routines. In line with this mission, their menu includes many varieties of facials, massages, skin-care services, and body wraps. There is a water-therapy room with a sauna and hot tub that are complimentary before or after your treatments. Yevgeniya's also specializes in nonsurgical face-lifts, acne facials, and microdermabrasion.

Yevgeniya's takes care of its customers with a custom spa-care line and a system to accumulate points for services. They also offer monthly seminars on antiaging and protective skin maintenance. It is clearly a place you will leave a little more knowledgeable each time you visit.

The Couple's Massage Lesson includes a Tension Relief Massage from the therapist as well as from your partner, so you can simultaneously relax, learn, and practice massage techniques together. The Tension Relief Massage includes upper-body work that focuses on the neck and shoulders, as well as a foot massage. What a great way to truly take your massage home!

The Total Wellness Treatment begins with a salt glow and massage. You will start by being surrounded in a tentlike apparatus from the neck down. The room will become steamy, and every so often a cold compress will be placed on your head and neck. The effect is detoxifying and not too hot, since the cold compresses create a cooling effect. Next, your skin, including your shoulders and neck, will be hydrated and massaged. The therapists are very educated and experienced, so you will feel deeply relaxed.

When you leave Yevgeniya's, you will have experienced a spa escape in a very cozy, homey atmosphere.

- Featured treatments: Couple's Massage Lesson, Total Wellness Treatment
- $10 off of a deluxe treatment
- Hours: Tue.–Sat. 10:00 AM–6:00 PM, Sun. & Mon. by appointment only

Yevgeniya's Russian Day Spa

The Spa at the Broadmoor

1 Lake Ave. • Colorado Springs, CO 80906

719-577-5770 • www.broadmoor.com

*You are invited to leave
your routine behind and rest
in the arms of grand luxury.*

The Broadmoor is a legendary five-star resort. Built in 1918, it features three golf courses, a tennis club, and a world-class spa. Yet despite the grounds' grandeur and size, the paths that wind through the 3,000 acres along with the hotel's transportation system create the feeling of being in a small town.

The Victorian decor puts you in a different time and place. In fact, at the Broadmoor you can imagine that you are anywhere in the world, as they are host to international guests and employees. You may feel as though you are on a faraway vacation as you are immediately whisked away into a state of relaxation.

Both the women's and men's locker areas feature a stream room, sauna, aromatherapy room, and fireplace room. There is also a room where you can join your spouse or friends to overlook the mountain vistas as you sip some warm tea. The resort's pool, hot tubs, and fitness facilities are available all day for spa patrons.

A highlight of The Spa at the Broadmoor is a TAG Studio–designed shower that is lovingly called "The Brain Scrub" by those who have experienced it. You may go in with troubles on your mind, but when you are done, you may not even remember your own name! This amazing shower can be a treatment by itself or an add-on to a service. You can choose from four different programs; 20 showerheads do the trick.

If you are nervous about wraps, it will only be a matter of minutes before the nervousness fades and comfort takes over. The Journey to Nirvana Wrap begins with an exfoliation process. During the wrap, you might experience what a baby feels when it is all wrapped up in blankets. The layers of the bed are designed to cocoon you, keeping you warm, cozy, and safe. You are then rinsed off by the Vichy shower. The Vichy shower plays an important role during this service. You never once have to leave the bed, and it is very comfortable. You may think you have now reached Nirvana, but there's still more: this treatment ends with a soothing face massage and scalp treatment.

The procedure for the Ashiatsu Deep Therapy treatment will be described to you thoroughly by your therapist. She first walks on your back from your toes to your neck. There is a point in this journey where the therapist works the shoulders and neck. You might assume she is using her hands, only to find out that she is still walking. She then massages your arms with her feet. This is not at all painful. As the therapist works out the knots and the massage gets deep, ujjayi breathing is recommended. This type of breathing involves the nostrils and the throat and assists in the process of calming the nervous system. The Ashiatsu Deep Therapy treatment can be done in a series to free troubled areas.

If it is luxury you are seeking, The Spa at the Broadmoor is likely to meet your needs with its wide array of services.

- Featured treatments: Journey to Nirvana Wrap, Ashiatsu Deep Therapy, TAG Shower
- 10% Discount
- Hours: Please call

The Spa at the Broadmoor

Jan Archuleta

West Central

<u>Summit County</u>

Blue Sage Spa

224 S. Main St. • Breckenridge, CO 80424

970-453-7676 • www.bluesagespa.com

*Whether you travel over Swan Mountain
or Hoosier Pass, a beautiful drive into the
mountain town of Breckenridge awaits you.*

Breckenridge is filled with year-round activities
and events, so no matter what your favorite
season is, you can find fun in this town. Shopping, skiing, biking, hiking, and, yes, spa-going
are just some of the ways to pass time here.

Main St. is full of restaurants and shops,
but, more importantly, here you will find Blue
Sage Spa, a wonderful retreat for those taking a
break from skiing or other outdoor adventures.
Don't pass by this spa, as you may think it is only
another storefront.

When you enter Blue Sage, you will find
that the hustle and bustle of Main St. soon disappears. Inside, time seems to stand still. The subdued lighting and the scent of the mildly fragrant

candles set the mood for your experience. The treatment rooms are located upstairs, toward the back of the spa. Be sure to enjoy the steam shower in the women's locker room.

Caren Mapes and Amy Beckett have been providing spa-goers a place to retreat for many years. They hire extremely knowledgeable and informed therapists who are very much in tune with body and skin-care needs. It is apparent that they are passionate about what they do as they pamper you during your entire visit. Choose from body treatments, massages, facials, and nail-care services. Put on a robe and enjoy yourself.

The Decadent Chocolate Therapy is just as it sounds—absolutely yummy! During this treatment, you will lie on a Hydrotone bed, which is a capsulelike shell that contains steam and shower capabilities so you do not need to get up to rinse. The service begins with a light brushing of your skin to whisk away dead cells. A chocolate-espresso scrub is then rubbed onto your body. Next, the top of the bed is lowered, encapsulating your body so it becomes wrapped in steam. While the steam works its magic, you will receive a head and neck massage from the therapist. You can feel the stress release as you enter a restful state. A Vichy shower follows the steam in order to rinse off the scrub. Afterward, while you are drying off, the therapist will prepare the bed for the second phase: a chocolate mask that moisturizes the skin.

You can even eat the mask! Although this therapy requires participation from you (because you will have to get up during the middle of the treatment to turn over), it is quite rewarding. A true sense of detoxification takes place as you feel the toxins leave your body. Your skin will feel replenished, and you will feel energetic once again.

The Blue Sage Facial is also a very rewarding treatment. Blue Sage Spa uses the Eminence line of products, which is organic and features a variety of scents to choose from. Karyn Blanco is a highly knowledgeable aesthetician who knows the right products for your skin's needs. From her, you will find out how the face can reveal information that may be helpful for the path to well-being. For example, breaking out on the forehead can sometimes be linked to the health of your kidneys, the cheek area to the liver, the mouth to digestive processes, and the jaw to hormones. When acne is stress related, the stress produces cortisol and increases oil on the dermal layer, resulting in clogged pores. But enough of this technical jargon—this facial is fun, smells and feels wonderful, and will make you ready to show off your natural beauty with great confidence. In addition to the facial, your hands will be treated to paraffin and warm hand mitts.

Take some extra time to enjoy the relaxation area. Here, you and your friends can chat, or you can just sit and rest, something none of us do often enough. You may even wish to have lunch. You can choose from items on a variety of menus from nearby restaurants, and your lunch will be ready for you after your service.

- Featured treatments: Decadent Chocolate Therapy, Blue Sage Facial
- 10% discount
- Hours: Daily 9:00 AM–9:00 PM

Serenity Spa & Salon

23110 US Hwy. 6, Ste. 116 • Keystone, CO 80435

800-910-0772 • www.serenitycolorado.com

Summer, winter, it doesn't matter—
Serenity is worth coming to in any season.

Summit County is home to Serenity Spa &
Salon, an Aveda establishment in a ski-resort
environment that is both welcoming and comfortable. This award-winning spa, adjacent to River
Run Village, is easily accessible for locals and
out-of-town visitors.

Behind the doors of Serenity, a sense of community fills the spa. The owner, Alina Stasiowski,
is committed to providing a spa that allows guests
to "experience the difference." In fact, the truth
behind this motto keeps you coming back to visit
again and again. Stasiowski has a global approach
to community, as Serenity sponsors events to help
raise funds for people around the world, and the
staff is very community and environmentally
conscious. The spa supports its neighborhood by
sponsoring festivals in the Keystone area and con-
tributing to the Summit Foundation. Although the
spa has a large returning international clientele,
Serenity could not survive without its local clients.

At Serenity, there is an extensive menu for men, women, and even teens that includes facials and nail- and hair-care services. You might see moms in the salon with their children, who are receiving routine haircuts; children ages 10 and under receive a complimentary cut. There is also a rewards system that allows clients to collect points toward free services. Nail care is performed in separate quarters, and the spa rooms are tucked in the back, allowing you to feel secluded. Here, you can enjoy a cup of tea or a glass of wine as you cozy up by the fireplace.

The oils used for treatments are based on the questionnaire that you are asked to fill out before your service. This information will help inform the therapist as to how you are feeling on that particular day. Massages are customized to each guest's needs, and when you schedule your service, you may request 50-, 60-, 75-, or 90-minute sessions. The Caribbean Therapy Body Treatment utilizes a detoxifying seaweed mask and includes a scalp and face massage. The Rosemary-Mint Awakening Body Wrap, a highly requested treatment, focuses on softening the skin with rosemary and peppermint and includes a scalp and foot massage.

Serenity is best known for its facials. Let us recommend the High-Altitude Hydrating Facial. This service incorporates antioxidants to help repair and protect your skin from Colorado's high-altitude environment. The treatment includes exfoliation, a hydrating mask, and massage. It is a mile-high (actually closer to two-mile-high) favorite!

The attention to detail at Serenity is impeccable. There is chocolate for you in your locker, and after your treatment, before exiting from the spa room, you are provided with lip gloss and a face spritz. Remember to enjoy a glass of wine in the fireplace lounge as you prolong entering reality.

- Featured treatment: High-Altitude Hydrating Facial
- 10% Discount
- Hours: Winter: Mon. 10:00 AM–6:00 PM, Tues.–Sat. 10:00 AM–8:00 PM, Sun. 11:00 AM–5:00 PM; Spring, summer, & fall: Mon.–Sat. 10:00 AM–6:00 PM

Aria Spa & Club

1300 Westhaven Dr. • Vail, CO 81657

888-824-5772 • www.vailcascade.com

Looking for fitness and pampering?
Choose Aria.

The Vail Valley invites you to step into a mountain escape with European flavor. Whether you take I-70 or the more scenic route through Breckenridge, there are plenty of opportunities to enjoy wildlife viewing and the breathtaking scenery.

Aria Spa & Club, part of the Vail Cascade Resort, blends fitness with massage in its own special way. Aria is set apart from other spas by its attention to detail, the immense size of its fitness facility and relaxation room, and the services it has to offer. You might be enticed to partake in all its recreational activities as well, which include swimming and racquetball.

At Aria, there is something for everyone. In fact, a whole family could enjoy a day here. The use of the fitness facility is free of charge on the day of your services, so Mom and Dad can enjoy treatments at the spa while the children enjoy a game of basketball. If there are little ones in the family, not to worry—Aria's child-care facility staff has 20 years of experience. Are you asking yourself, where is the relaxation with all this activity around? Again, not to worry! Upstairs in the spa you are far removed from the noise down below.

Aria features an extensive menu that will please all. The spa, which is over 10,000 square feet, consists of 14 spa rooms, a couple's suite, and a separate area for manicures and pedicures that features a pipeless system to minimize the risk of infections. Aria's Songs of the Mountains are special packages worth trying. Combinations include hiking, snowshoeing, yoga, or Pilates along with selected spa services and even a glass of wine.

The enormous yet cozy sanctuary room offers the perfect spot for taking a nap, enjoying a book, or just sipping a fine cup of tea. Tea lovers will appreciate the thoughtfulness of the spa in providing fresh tea leaves to steep in individual tea presses. Make a perfect cup to savor before or after your treatment and relax while warming yourself by the centrally located fireplace.

Treat yourself to the Neem Body Wrap. This wrap is a cleansing and hydrating service that encourages the body's own natural healing process while replacing lost nourishment. The Neem Balance Wrap with Scalp Treatment is truly set apart from traditional wraps and warrants the experience. It includes the use of the Hydrotable, which originated in Germany and was first used for physical therapy. The therapist stated that "the floating effect of the water takes the pressure of gravity off the spine, and the heat activates the treatment." The sensation of being lowered is a little awkward, but soon you are enrobed with such warmth and security you won't want to be raised again. The wrap is followed by a massage and scalp treatment that leaves your skin well nourished.

The people play an integral role at this spa. There is a family and community oriented feeling at Aria. With highly trained and experienced therapists on staff, this spa is sure to be on your list of favorites. From the treatments offered to the exceptional service you will receive to the relaxing atmosphere, Aria is the perfect place in which to immerse yourself in the holistic pampering of your mind and body.

- Featured treatment: Neem Balance Wrap
- 10% discount
- Hours: Winter: Daily 9:00 AM–8:00 PM; Summer: Daily 9:00 AM–7:00 PM

Allegria Spa

100 E. Thomas Pl. • Beaver Creek, CO 81620

970-748-7500 • www.allegriaspa.com

Enjoy a trip to the Allegria Spa,
a ski-in and ski-out location.

Travel west on I-70 to Allegria Spa, which is located in the Park Hyatt Beaver Creek Resort. The recently renovated spa and resort are surrounded by a European-like village that offers ample shopping and entertainment options throughout the year, and the Park Hyatt itself offers children's programs and family-oriented activities during both the summer and winter seasons. Allegria even offers a treatment called the Prima Donna especially for little divas ages 8 to 12.

Gaye Steinke, general manager, has restructured the Allegria into a contemporary facility that pays homage to the ancient roots of the spa. Entering the two-story, 30,000-square-foot facility, you will find a large reception area and a boutique for your shopping pleasure. Allegria has been aligned with feng shui practices in mind. The spa is decorated with native flora and fauna. The spa rooms are above ground, allowing for the natural light to provide ambience. The locker rooms are spacious and offer all the amenities you need to complete your spa experience.

The spa has a fitness center that offers Pilates, yoga, free weights, treadmills, and bikes for your workout. Use of the pools, hot tubs, and fitness facility is free of charge to spa guests. Allegria offers special discounts to members for treatments and personal training.

Allegria is one of three spas in Colorado that have a kinesis program. Kinesis is a type of training that originated in Italy. Here, you can practice it with a private instructor or participate in one of the classes offered. Kinesis is extremely helpful for skiing and improving your golf swing, as it uses fluid movement in order to work muscles in all areas.

Allegria features a heated outdoor pool, which is tucked into the hills, along with outdoor hot tubs, a dry sauna, and a steam room. An extensive spa menu offers special packages if you want to spend hours away from reality, such as the Rocky Mountain Cures, which exfoliate and detoxify the body, as well as a variety of global therapies such as Ashiatsu and Thai massage. The spa also offers salon services and several treatments for teens and men.

Experience the wondrous Ginger-Peach Cure. Ground ginger, orange peel, raw sugar, and essential nut oils are combined to complete the scrub.

After your shower, a honey-and-ginger mask is applied with a massage. You are then wrapped in warm blankets and treated to a scalp massage.

The Aqua Sanitas is an enriching add-on to any treatment. Whether you do this before or after your service, it is quite extraordinary. Translated as "healing waters," Aqua Sanitas is a sequence of water therapies that date back to the ancient Roman baths. Aqua Sanitas alternates temperatures that calm and rejuvenate your soul. First, you'll shower and then go to the sanctuary. Next, you'll take a dip in the Thermae Mineral Pool. This natural-springs pool (which is coed) has juniper mineral salts that raise your temperature and increase blood circulation. They can also increase your metabolism and heal sore muscles. You'll follow up with the Caldarium Pool, which is a warm pool with wildflower aromatherapy. Next, the Cascata Rain Shower will make you feel as though you are caught in the most exquisite cool downpour. This is a wonderful transition from the warm pool—but you are not done yet. Next, you'll move into the Caldarium Steam Room, which is filled with the scent of spruce. Tiny colored lights blink in a pattern above. Wow! The final step is the Tepidarium. Here, you'll relax in heated lounge chairs and breathe in an herbal mist.

Allegria is Italian for "blissful," and after spending some time here, you will experience the true meaning of this spa.

- Featured treatments: Ginger-Peach Cure,
  Aqua Sanitas
- Hours: Winter: Daily 8:00 AM–8:00 PM;
  Summer: Daily 8:00 AM–7:00 PM

The Spa at Cordillera

2205 Cordillera Way • Edwards, CO 81632

970-569-6359 • www.cordilleralodge.com

$$$

*With its awe-inspiring vistas and
wonderful treatments, Cordillera will take
you on a journey to relaxation.*

We are not done with the Vail Valley yet.
Travel even farther on I-70 to Edwards,
and a pleasant surprise awaits you at the Cordil-
lera. Unique chateaulike construction highlights
the hotel's grandeur. The spa was built in 1989
and has gone through several renovations since,
all the while maintaining European decor com-
bined with natural earth tones to bring the out-
doors in. Plan to stay a few days, as you will
want to experience the feel of an exclusive, pri-
vate getaway.

The Spa at Cordillera sets itself apart with
its skilled and dedicated staff and a location that
is breathtaking. Several therapists have been here
for more than 10 years, and guests come here year
after year for the deluxe accommodations.

The spa itself occupies the first floor of the
hotel. It features a fitness center, a room for yoga
and meetings, a lap pool, and indoor and outdoor

hot tubs. There are eight treatment rooms and two facial rooms. Three hotel rooms have direct access to the spa. But even with all these amenities, you may find yourself simply napping in the relaxation room, as this space provides the perfect tranquil setting.

The Spa at Cordillera offers body treatments, massages, and skin- and nail-care services for men and women. Classes and services such as fitness evaluations for body composition, blood pressure, and resting heart rate entice locals as well as tourists. Cordillera's goal is to customize treatments. The therapists promote wellness with fitness, nutrition, and spa services. Here, clients can learn how to reach their goals of living a healthier lifestyle.

The Spirit of Cordillera is a very relaxing massage and hydrating body wrap. It will loosen up sore muscles and help heal the dry skin that is ever so common in our arid climate. A scalp massage enhances and complements this treatment. You will leave feeling quite revived and ready to share a lively dinner while reminiscing with friends.

The Ultraluxe Age-Control Facial will leave your skin radiant and rejuvenated. This 80-minute treatment does not involve any extractions. Nine antiaging ingredients blend together to form the spa's signature Hydrating ProPeel, which is infused with papaya and oat protein.

Cordillera may seem far away from Denver, but it really isn't. The ambiance at this destination spa truly takes you away to pure rest.

- Featured treatment: The Spirit of Cordillera
- 10% discount
- Hours: Daily 8:00 AM–8:00 PM
  (Can be seasonal, so call ahead)

Splendor Mountain Day Spa

506 Maple St. • Glenwood Springs, CO 81601

970-945-7454 • www.splendormtndayspa.com

$

*Looking for an experience that
awakens all of your senses?
Try Splendor Mountain Day Spa.*

Three hours west of Denver, just off of 1-70, sits Glenwood Springs, known as the home of the world's largest hot springs. Taking the train has been a relaxing option for visitors traveling from Denver to Glenwood for over 100 years, but whether you are peering out the window of the Glenwood Springs train or the window of your own car, it's a scenic trip as you watch the greenery of the mountains become a desertlike red.

Glenwood Springs is an old town with a lot of character, and the setting is reminiscent of the Old West. Images of the infamous Doc Holliday, who died here more than a century ago, are painted on the small buildings throughout the town. One of the nicest things about Glenwood Springs is that recreation and restaurants are within easy walking distance. If you would like more of a physical challenge, try biking through the canyon or hiking at Hanging Lake.

In contrast to the tourist attractions, Splendor Mountain Day Spa offers the gift of true respite. This is a small, quiet spa that comprises four rooms, including an aesthetician's room, couple's room, and a therapy pool. If you are not interested in a massage or any of the other treatments offered, you are still invited to come and visit, rest on the comfortable couch, and sip tea. Upon entering this spa, you feel the serenity of the environment inviting you to take a moment to stop and quiet your busy thoughts.

It is clear that the owners and therapists are here because they love what they do. Giving to others through focused treatments is not the only aspect of the community that Splendor Mountain is involved in. This spa donates treatments to various causes and even features clothing for sale that profits a women's group in South America.

The mission of Splendor Mountain is to connect with people through their senses. Massage appeals to the sense of touch, allowing you to unwind. The aroma of nature's own healing fragrances of herbs, clays, salts, and oils engages the sense of smell. The sounds of a local musician, guitarist Steve Jueneman, fill the air. The sight of well-tended gardens, fresh flowers, and soothing colors adds ambiance. And the taste of the freshly brewed, exquisitely blended herbal tea completes the sensual journey.

Opened in 1998 by Susan Wilmot, Splendor Mountain is now lovingly tended by a trio of owners: mother, daughter, and sister. Ruth Sears and Rebekah Apodaca joined Splendor Mountain in 2003. Together, they feature the most comprehensive menu of treatments on the Western Slope. It includes Thai massage, Rolfing, Ashiatsu, Watsu, water dance, and more.

Do not miss an opportunity to have Watsu, which can be described as a warm, exquisite liquid journey. Feel yourself unwind as your body is stretched, massaged, rocked, and released in the unique therapy pool.

If you have tried Watsu and found it to be blissful, you may want to experience the underwater realm of water dance. Water dance is similar to Watsu, but you will move below the surface of the water to experience a deeper state of relaxation. Follow Watsu or water dance with a massage, as your muscles will be warm and receptive.

This serene spa offers services that will help you to reach a state of renewal.

- Featured treatments: Watsu, Water dance
- 10% discount
- Hours: Daily 10:00 am–7:00 pm
  by appointment only

Yampah Spa & Salon
The Hot Springs Vapor Caves

709 E. 6th St. • Glenwood Springs, CO 81601

970-945-0667 • www.yampahspa.com

$$

*Looking for an experience that is built
around nature? The Hot Springs Vapor
Caves are not to be missed.*

This spa actually protects a natural resource. Dating back to 1893, the Yampah Spa & Salon was built around vapor caves. The caves are accessible to the public for a nominal fee or complimentary if you have a treatment at the spa. Native Americans can access the caves free of charge, as this area is part of their heritage and a sacred place for meditation. They often use the caves for sweats at night, when the facilities are closed to the public.

Plan extra time and bring a friend the first time you venture down into the 124°F caves—the feeling of doing so can be reminiscent of stepping down into a basement as a child and not knowing what is going to greet you. Although the caves are only one flight down and there is a railing, the journey is steep, and the steps are made of rock, so the trip is not recommended for those who do not have sure footing or can't see well without glasses or contacts. But all warnings aside, this is an experience you will remember forever and come to again and again. It is like being ultimately relaxed and having all of your senses heightened at the same time.

Some interesting things happen down in the caves. When we visited, there were people talking quietly, cuddling, stretching, and just breathing to take in the vapors that detoxify the body. There are people who love the caves more than the hot springs themselves. Customers often leave saying that they feel like they have "silky lungs."

The pure, clean water of the hot mineral baths are another favorite among guests. The baths are a nice size and a welcome private retreat for individuals or couples.

The feel of the spa itself is natural and rustic. There is a beautiful circular solarium where both male and female guests wait in comfortable lightweight robes for their therapists to greet them. Straight-back and lounge chairs are provided, along with reading material and lemon water. With walls painted light green and soft light streaming in through the ceiling, you may find that this is a nice place in which to sit and relax for an hour or so.

The locker rooms are much like those at your local pool in that they are open, and opportunities for privacy are scarce, so those of you who are modest will need to plan time to go to the restroom first to change and then come back to the locker room. Don't forget a quarter to lock up all of your belongings. A hair dryer and mirror are provided, and there is ample room in which to reapply your makeup before reentering the world.

If you are having salon services, it is important to know that the salon is located up two flights of stairs and is more easily accessible than the caves. The spa and salon offer a complete menu that includes hair services, hand and foot treatments, facials, herbal baths, and numerous body and massage treatments. There is even an Oxygen Experience where you are hooked up to an oxygen tank for 25 minutes. It alleviates altitude sickness, headaches, and more. This is a wonderful way to relax your mind and body simultaneously.

The wraps at Yampah are not for those who mind baring it all. Unlike at other spas, you won't be covered first and then wrapped. Instead, you will be asked to remove your clothing first, and then the wrap is applied while you are in all your glory. The therapist helps apply the product or blankets. It does not feel invasive or strange as long as you remember to release your worries about being au naturel.

However, massage etiquette is more traditional. The therapist leaves the room while you get undressed, then, once the massage begins, she covers the other parts of your body while she focuses on a specific part for the massage. The massage rooms are separated by curtains instead of doors, so remember to keep talking to a minimum. The Herbal Wrap combined with a massage is an excellent and affordable two hours of pampering. Check the website or ask about the monthly specials, which are great deals. Yampah Spa & Salon is nature at its finest.

- Featured treatments: Herbal Wrap, Massage
- Hours: Daily 9:00 AM–9:00 PM

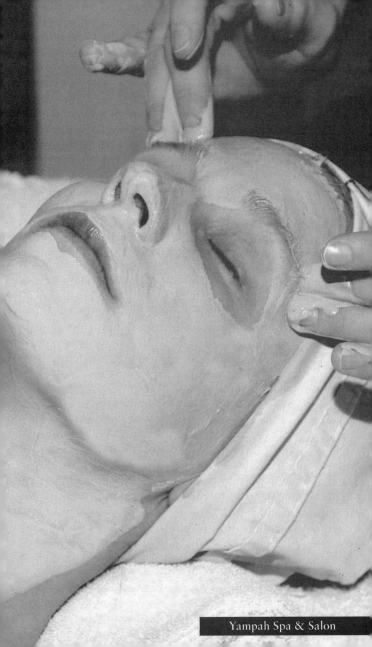

The Aspen Club & Spa

1450 Ute Ave. • Aspen, CO 81611

866-484-8254 • www.aspenclub.com

$$$ 🏋

*Are you looking for a spa with innovative
ideas, extensive facilities, and a
community minded feeling?
If so, Aspen Club & Spa is for you.*

Nestled in the heart of Aspen, The Aspen
Club & Spa has promoted wellness for
more than 30 years. It is a members-only club,
but all types of memberships are available,
whether you desire a one-time visit, a yearly vaca-
tion, or plan to come every day. It is a large facil-
ity that features a swimming pool, steam rooms,
and whirlpools. It also has a sports medicine
clinic with physical therapists, certified personal
trainers, and chiropractors on staff.

The spa offers salon services as well as nail,
body, and facial care. The sanctuary is a wonder-
ful place for relaxing while sipping tea or water
and eating fresh fruit. You will want to arrive
early to take full advantage of this tranquil space
prior to your appointment.

The Ashiatsu treatment is a deep-tissue
massage that promises to work out any troubled

areas. During this service, the therapist holds onto bars on the ceiling above you and walks on your back. This process helps release knots, and you will soon succumb to deep relaxation. The areas of your neck, shoulders, arms, legs, and scalp will not be ignored, as they are then massaged by the therapist's hands. This treatment can be very deep and rejuvenating.

The Alpine Rejuvenator is a revitalizing body treatment. Your service begins with a steam towel compress used over the entire body. A body scrub is then applied, followed by a mask of rich botanicals, and then a wrap. This treatment culminates with an application of pine essential oils that are indigenous to the region.

Another highlight is the Oxygen Treatment, which fully hydrates and restores your skin. Oxygen enriched with 87 vitamins, minerals, amino acids, and enzymes is propelled into the dermal layer. This treatment can be done as an add-on to a facial or all alone. Your skin will thank you.

Future plans at The Aspen Club & Spa include building a five-acre holistic-health community called Aspen Club Living. It will be geothermally heated and will focus on reduced energy consumption. Aspen Club Living will be the first environmentally sustainable neighborhood in the United States that families can return to for their annual retreat. Check the website for updates.

- Featured treatments: Ashiatsu, Alpine Rejuvinator, Oxygen Treatment
- 10% discount
- Hours: Daily 6:00 AM–9:00 PM

SOUTH CENTRAL

SAN LUIS VALLEY

Joyful Journey Hot Springs Spa

28640 CR 58 EE • Moffat, CO 81143

719-256-4328 • www.joyfuljourneyhotsprings.com

*In the middle of nowhere, there is a
treasure waiting to be discovered.*

There is nothing that compares to a road trip with a few of your friends. Travel on Hwy. 285 south from Denver to Moffat and find Joyful Journey awaiting your long overdue arrival. Whether you are coming up from the Southwest or traveling down to the sand dunes, Joyful Journey is worth a stop. Enjoy overnight accommodations or visit for a few hours to soak in the pools and have a treatment before you hit the road again.

Joyful Journey has recently expanded. It now offers hotel-style lodging in addition to yurts, teepees, and camping facilities. The yurts are very spacious, comfortable, and heated. A conference room is available for special gatherings such as weddings, reunions, and yoga classes. Spa rooms can be found in the lodging facility for additional treatments and alternative healing modalities. And there will be two more pools in the near future, one of which will be specially designed for Watsu.

This spa has been family owned since 1987. Elaine Blumenhein brings her nursing and caregiving background to the mission of the spa. She takes pride in being able to share the gift of healing waters with everyone. Joyful Journey takes advantage of the area's geothermal waters by assigning different pools different temperatures to accommodate all types of visitors. All of the pools are drained and cleaned every night. The waters, which do not have a sulfurous odor, are rich with lithium, which helps transport sodium and potassium to nerves in the brain and muscles.

The Crystal Age-Reversing Facial will leave you feeling hydrated and pampered. After a deep-cleansing process, the therapist will apply POMÉ Crystals to your face. Annaé Geoceuticals in Boulder claims that POMÉ Crystals, which are a blend of more than 45 crystals, activate the skin's ability to return to its original state. The crystals tend to itch, but you will be busy concentrating on how good the reflexology feels on your legs, feet, arms, and hands. You will then enjoy a heavenly scalp massage, taking you further into a pool of tranquility. After the scalp massage, the crystals are removed with hot towels. This process will leave your skin feeling soft again.

The Native Blanket Wrap is an enriched exfoliation treatment that uses Indian tobacco, espresso, sarsaparilla, and soothing herbs. It is detoxifying and hydrating. This service involves meridian stretching and finger pressure combined with the Rolfing technique. Rolfing integrates myofascial therapy with the manipulation of soft tissues to provide an overall sense of well-being and proper alignment. It works with the layers of muscles but extends the benefits to your joints and bones as well, leaving you satisfied and feeling very flexible.

At Joyful Journey, you may feel as though you are surrounded by timeless space. During your visit, take in a breath of fresh air as you sit on Meditation Hill and enjoy the serene landscape.

- Featured treatments: Crystal Age-Reversing Facial, Native Blanket Wrap
- 10% discount
- Hours: Daily 10:00 AM–10:00 PM

Joyful Journey Hot Springs Spa

Spa Sola Fidé

38 Ben Eaton Ln. • Rosita Hills • Westcliffe, CO 81252

877-783-4270 • www.spasolafide.com

If the seclusion of a couple's
retreat appeals to you,
find your way to Spa Sola Fidé.

A visit to Spa Sola Fidé brings you to one of the most pristine parts of our state. Heading southwest from Colorado Springs through a red-rock valley, the landscape alternates between wooded mountains and open space. After an easy 90 miles, you will find yourself on the verge of the Sangre de Cristo Mountains at an elevation of 8,400 feet. Surrounded by wildlife and ponderosa pines, Spa Sola Fidé provides you with a secluded retreat. Located only 10 miles from Westcliffe, restaurants, shops, rafting, horseback riding, fishing, and more can be found nearby.

Opened in 2003, Spa Sola Fidé is a labor of love for Guy and Karen Madden. *Sola fidé* is Latin for "by faith alone." It is an expression of the Maddens' spiritual beliefs and their willingness to leave security behind and start life again with a new vision. They hope to maintain an intimate setting where couples can focus on a time of reconnection, renewal, and rest without the intrusions of technology.

This 760-square-foot cottage has been handcrafted with a native beetle-kill pine ceiling and Douglas fir floor and trim. Offering casual elegance and a Southwestern motif, it is romantic, charming, and cozy. The warmth from the stove, sounds of the fountain, and smells of the forest pine are wonderful accompaniments to the expansive views of the mountains.

Massages are by appointment only and thus very flexible in terms of the types of treatments offered and the length of your service. The treatment room is within the cottage. Natural light pours in through two windows; these can be opened to the sound of chirping birds to add to your relaxation. Several types of massages are available, and there is even a health assessment.

The Japanese Anma Facial is not for skin care, but rather for muscle relaxation. It is an ancient form of facial massage that eliminates headaches and neck aches, and leaves you in a Zen-like state of relaxation. It combines light strokes and pressure-point massage with aromatherapy and breathing techniques to release muscle tension and allow you to better accommodate the natural ebbs and flows of life.

The integrated hot-stone massage and Ashiatsu Oriental bar therapy uses hot stones to soothe stressed muscles, open up energy chakras, and increase circulation. A blanket of stones is placed on your back while others are used along your body. You can feel the heat preparing your body for the Ashiatsu. The therapist then uses her feet for deeper compression to release sore aches and pains. This technique provides the client with increased range of motion and a new sense of physical freedom. After this treatment, even the most talkative among you may find yourselves speechless!

The Health Assessment is exclusive to Spa Sola Fidé. Conducted by Karen, who has 32 years of experience as a registered nurse, this service is a focused discussion to create awareness of your daily well-being. It does not feel as though you are in a doctor's office, but rather visiting with a friend who listens to your goals and the pressures of your life. You will leave with resources to combat stress and bring balance to your life. It is a wonderful accompaniment that adds a focus on holistic care.

- Featured treatments: Japanese Anma Facial, Hot Stone–Ashiatsu Oriental Bar Therapy Combination Massage, Health Assessment
- 10% discount
- Hours: Daily by appointment only

SOUTHWEST

DURANGO

Trimble Spa
& Natural Hot Springs

6475 CR 203 • Durango, CO 81302

970-247-0212 • www.trimblehotsprings.com

*The Anasazi called this land home
and carved their lives from the
natural resources they found here.*

There are several ways to reach Durango from Denver, but you will not want to miss the San Juan Skyway. At just over 11,000 feet at the summit, this is one of the most scenic drives in the world. On this journey, you will witness the wonders of Mother Nature and her abundance of flora and fauna.

Seven miles north of downtown Durango, in the Animas Valley, you will want to find yourself at Trimble Spa & Natural Hot Springs. The healing waters in this area have been in existence for over 1,000 years. The resort received its name in the late 1800s from Frank Trimble. Trimble was a soldier in the American Indian Wars and suffered from rheumatism. He considered himself healed after bathing in these waters for some time and later built a two-story hotel here. Although it burned down, over the decades to come the hotel was reincarnated in many other forms, including a Victorian-style home and a dude ranch. People claimed that the Indians had cursed the place, and it was left alone for nearly 30 years in the late 1900s. Finally, there was another attempt to rebuild, but this time the Southern Ute tribe was invited to attend the opening ceremonies. At that time, their spiritual leader blessed the grounds for the new Trimble Hot Springs.

In June 2006, Patrick J. McIvor and a group of local investors purchased the facility. They are currently in the process of renovating the resort. Their vision is to "develop Trimble to its full potential as a destination resort with an emphasis on wellness, while also providing public access at reasonable prices."

At Trimble, you will find locals enjoying the day at the naturally heated pools and picnicking on the lawn. The spa is located behind the pools, somewhat secluded by a fence separating it from the rest of the area. Originally a private residence, the spa has a kitchen where the therapists can blend their own essential oils for treatments. The spa features a pool for guests to soak in, the Red Rock Pool, which is a natural source of mineral-rich geothermal water. Trimble is also proud of its Sunlight Studio, a great location for yoga and tai chi classes, and the Starlight Suite, a romantic spot for a special celebration.

The spa offers a variety of services, including herbal oil wraps, salt glows, and therapeutic massages. Salt glows and herbal oil wraps are body treatments that leave your skin feeling soft and awakened. If you can't choose, try one of the very popular combinations.

Many of the therapists here specialize in LaStone therapy. This 90-minute ancient bodywork technique alternates warm basalt riverbed stones and chilled marble to promote deep relaxation. LaStone relaxes the muscles in a different process than a traditional massage. It incorporates the alignment of chakras, and additional benefits include stimulation of the circulatory system, pain reduction, restoration of balance to the body, and the clearance of toxins. The hot and cold stones provide the sensation of being under a cool waterfall in a tropical paradise. Soothe your body's tensions and release your worries with this treatment.

Watch Trimble Spa & Natural Hot Springs in the future, as plans for expansion are well under way. There are designs for rebuilding a facsimile of the Hermosa House, which was a Victorian three-story brick building that was built in 1896 and served as a resort before burning down in 1931. Trimble is on its way to becoming a world-class resort spa-and-hotel destination. Currently, it is the only hot springs/spa experience in the Durango area.

- Featured treatment: LaStone Therapy
- 10% discount
- Hours: Fall: Mon.–Thurs. 11:00 AM–7:00 PM,
  Fri. & Sat. 9:00 AM–8:00 PM,
  Sun. 9:00 AM–7:00 PM;
  Spring and winter:
  Sun.–Thurs. 10:00 AM–9:00 PM,
  Fri. & Sat. 10:00 AM–10:00 PM

Trimble Spa & Natural Hot Springs

The Historic Wiesbaden Hot Springs Spa and Lodgings

625 5th St. • Ouray, CO 81427

970-325-4347 • www.wiesbadenhotsprings.com

The Wiesbaden is a mecca of relaxation, complete rest, and spiritual bliss

Ouray lies at the head of the Uncompahgre Valley and is surrounded by mountains. It offers a mix of ruggedness and beauty. Long before the mining industry came into play, the Ute Indians resided in this part of the country. Ouray was named for Chief Ouray, the leader of the Uncompahgre Utes. In fact, one of the cabins of the Wiesbaden sits directly atop the ruins of Chief Ouray's mountain home.

The history of the Wiesbaden is fascinating. It began as Mother Buchanan's Bathhouse in 1879. In the 1920s, Dr. C. V. Bates established Bates Hospital here. The history of the Wiesbaden is sketchy between the 1940s and 1970s, until Linda Wright-Minter purchased it in 1978 and made the resort what it is today. The Ute Indians consider these springs sacred and deem them miracle waters. They are still used for ceremonial purposes.

For overnight accommodations, choose from individual rooms in the bed-and-breakfast, a cottage on the hill, an apartment, or a large three-bedroom, two-bath Victorian replica, as well as a small house; both the Victorian replica and small house are listed on the historic register.

The Wiesbaden boasts a natural vapor cave, an outdoor pool, and a secluded private outdoor hot tub, called the Lorelei, for guests' relaxation and enjoyment. The hot springs that feed these soaking facilities are untreated with chemicals and additives, leaving the medicinal and healing qualities of the springs and their world-renowned therapeutic properties intact. The temperatures of the pools vary from 100°F to 109°F, with the vapor cave being the hottest, at 107°F to 109°F. From the Lorelei and outdoor pool, take in the majestic views of the Twin Peaks and White House. As you enter the spa rooms downstairs, take note of the warm floors, as the springs naturally provide radiant heat.

Wright-Minter, who is the definition of a visionary, has owned Wiesbaden for over 30 years. She believes there is a need to return to basics. Wright-Minter appreciates what nature has to offer: "respecting and maintaining the natural evolution of the Wiesbaden" is her philosophy. Beyond the composition and properties of the water, there exists a spiritual energy here that emits a sense of healing and peace. Schedule a massage, reflexology treatment, dry brushing, LaStone therapy, or mud wrap while staying at the Wiesbaden.

The Swedish Massage is customized to meet your particular needs and release the tension from your body. The therapists are all very well trained and experienced. You will feel at ease and relaxed from all your worries as this massage works to the very fibers of your being.

The Mud Wrap treatment tightens pores, improves circulation, and helps sore muscles. You might feel like Silly Putty as you are lightly massaged and wrapped in warm mud. Wrinkles and skin flaws are often created by toxins; wraps can remove these toxins. This service is both detoxifying and uplifting.

People from all over the world come to the Wiesbaden to bathe and experience the curative powers of these healing hot springs. Why not come and indulge in them yourself?

- Featured treatments: Swedish Massage, Mud Wrap
- First-time lodging guests who refer to *Colorado Spas* will receive a complimentary hour for two in the Lorelei private outdoor spa and 10 percent off lodging during the Winter Season Special, which runs from November 15

to May 15. Restrictions do apply, so please inquire when making reservations.

- Hours: Winter: Sun.–Thurs. 8:00 AM–8:45 PM, Fri. & Sat. 8:00 AM–9:45 PM; Summer: Daily 8:00 AM–9:45 PM

Wiesbaden Hot Springs Spa

Chipeta Sun Lodge & Spa

304 S. Lena St. • Ridgway, CO 81432

970-626-3737 • www.chipeta.com

*Chipeta is blessed with natural surround-
ings. You will feel internally and externally
blessed after a visit to this inspiring retreat.*

Make Chipeta Sun Lodge & Spa your next
destination. The name of this spa honors
the wife of Chief Ouray. The adobe architecture
creates a serene atmosphere that provides comfortable yet elegant surroundings. The resort
features accommodations in the lodge, Chipeta
condominiums, and the Kiva Suites. Some of
these rooms come with their own private hot tub
on a balcony. The resort even has its own restau-
rant, the Four Corners Cafe, which specializes in
Southwestern cuisine.

Inspired by natural beauty and the surrounding mountains, Chipeta Sun Lodge & Spa
offers a place for personal growth and spiritual
well-being. Everything about this lodge and spa
promotes a sense of wellness. Locals frequent the
fitness center, also known as the Kiva, to work
toward a healthier lifestyle. Use of the Kiva is
free to spa guests. There are also two hot tubs

to choose from. Additionally, the spa offers a meditative retreat that manifests spiritual well-being. Services here include whole-body treatments, skin care, and massage therapies for men and women. Special packages include retreats for couples and girlfriend getaways, and some even include yoga sessions.

The spa features ISUN, a line of organic skin-care products. The creators of ISUN have integrated traditional knowledge and advanced energy science into their plant-based products. The active ingredients work into the skin at the cellular level as they restore purity.

Owners Patsy and Jack Young's mission is to allow people to remove themselves from their normally busy environments to one with a higher vibration and spiritual awakening. The spa is the heart of the resort and plays an integral role, as it honors original ancestors of the land and their traditions. Enjoy some time in the garden, where you can meditate in the "way-gones" before or after your services. The way-gone is Jack's rendition of a Native American hogan, traditionally a spot for spiritual quests.

The staff is friendly and knowledgeable, and the therapists at the spa are intuitive. They listen to the messages from your body and focus their energy work on areas that beg for it. The art of massage is very ceremonious here and focused on the mind-body connection.

The Feather Massage is a wonderful representation of honoring tradition. A wisp of a feather lightly touched to your bare skin before the massage prompts your circulation into action. This provides a lymphatic cleansing and prepares you for a state of receiving. Some people refer to this state as a spiritual awakening, or reaching a higher plane. The feather is also a symbolic reminder to stay on the high road and focus on what truly matters for the future, as the energy you carry will return you to the source of your existence. The massage continues with a coconut oil blend that may leave you feeling enlightened.

The Spa Facial is quite an educational experience. The therapist informs you of the appropriate steps for your skin-care needs based on the condition of your skin: dry, oily, or normal. You will feel relaxed and taken away to another realm as your skin is left replenished and glowing once again. This facial is very balancing.

If you are lucky enough to visit the Fiji Islands, don't forget to put Chipeta's sister spa, Rainforest Spa at Koro Sun Resort, on your go-to list. There, you will be surrounded by the sound of waterfalls, as the spa is located on a stream in the rain forest.

- Featured treatments: Feather Massage, Spa Facial
- 10% discount
- Hours: Daily 7:00 AM–8:00 PM

Atmosphere Spa

PO Box 3741 • 250 W. San Juan Ave. • Telluride, Colorado 81435

970-728-0630 • www.telluridespa.com

$$$

Kick off those ski boots
and slip on some sandals.

Whichever season you travel to Telluride, take time to enjoy the natural splendor. The roads are a bit twisty but far from treacherous, and the views of the spruce-covered mountains are magnificent. A historic 19th-century mining town, Telluride is best known today for its year-round athletic appeal, ski resort for all levels, and the annual film festival.

The town of Telluride, with its Victorian-era architecture, is only 6 blocks wide and 12 blocks long. One of the best things about it is that you will not need a car to get wherever you need to go. While you are here, make sure to visit Colorado's longest free-falling waterfall, the 365-foot Bridal Veil Falls, which is just east of town.

Located at the base of the gondola in the Camel's Garden Hotel, Atmosphere Spa is a destination for relaxation. You can ski, eat, sleep, and spa all in one spot.

It is a small spa with treatment rooms set around a comfortable waiting area decorated in a modern style. The purple and yellow colors are uplifting, making this spa a fun environment as well as a renewing one. A large window allows natural light and fresh air into the room. Tea and lemon water are available, and there is very comfortable seating. In one of their oh-so-comfortable rooms, you might just fall asleep after a day of activity.

The personalities of the therapists are an added element to this spa. Several of them are from other countries, and their different methods and knowledge about treatments are refreshing.

Atmosphere Spa offers facials, massages, body treatments, hand and foot care, and more. There are two different spa packages, the Remedy Relaxation and the Soul Sampler, if you would like to try all that Atmosphere has to offer.

Another fun aspect of this spa is that they will deliver a spa party to you. Both massage and beauty services are available. A spa party coordinator will walk you through the planning process.

The Holistic Green Coffee Wrap is a metabolism-lifting, slimming, and toning body wrap. When you hear that it is a slimming wrap in addition to being rejuvenating, you will not want to pass it up. It is recommended for those who might be feeling sluggish. Coffee is massaged all over your body, followed by an extensive Vichy shower and nourishing aromatherapy massage. But please note: this is not a treatment for those who are shy.

Several types of facials are available at Atmosphere, including the Multivitamin Facial, the Environmental Control Facial, and the Acne Corrective Facial; however, the Atmosphere Customized Facial is always a great choice as it is tailored to your specific skin type and needs. This service is geared toward both effective skin care and relaxation, and includes cleansing, toning, exfoliation, extractions, massage, and a mask. The goal is to thoroughly take care of your skin and leave it radiant and healthy looking.

If you are looking for a modern, uplifting spa, you will be happy at Atmosphere.

- Featured treatments: Holistic Green Coffee Wrap, Atmosphere Customized Facial
- Hours: Daily 9:00 AM–7:00 PM

Golden Door Spa
at the Peaks Resort

136 Country Club Dr. • Telluride, CO 81435

970-728-2590 • www.thepeaksresort.com

*Are you ready to visit a spa
with a breathtaking view?
Visit Golden Door Spa at the Peaks.*

Set in Mountain Village just above Telluride
with the San Juan Mountains as the backdrop,
the Golden Door Spa at the Peaks Resort boasts a
view like no other. The truly astonishing scenery
can be further enjoyed by riding the gondola in
Telluride to and from the spa.

Inspired by the ancient Honjin inns of Japan,
Deborah Szekely created the original Golden
Door Spa in 1958. Today, the Golden Door Spas
continue in the tradition of these inns to discern
guests' needs and restore their spirit and energy
through a complete personal well-being program.
The Golden Door Spa at the Peaks incorporates
a variety of techniques and ingredients from
Europe and the Far East as well as traditions of
the Southern Utes, who once made their home in
this spectacular mountain setting.

The most expansive and luxurious spa in the

area, the Golden Door Spa at the Peaks debuted a $2 million renovation in fall of 2007. The intent was to create a holistic experience, and there was a refocus of the core philosophy, which is to balance mind, body, and spirit. Golden Door strives to provide an exclusive sanctuary where members of the community and resort guests can integrate wellness into every aspect of their lives.

The spa is tranquil and Zen-like. The space flows seamlessly from reception to lounge to treatment room. Both men and women have every amenity imaginable here. Make sure to take advantage of the hot tub, steam room, and sauna.

The Ritual-for-Two Massage begins with a footbath and a few minutes alone to talk and enjoy the moment while you sit on a couch facing a window. Then the massage begins. The tables are arranged so that they are facing one another instead of side by side. This makes for a very nice experience that can be shared with either a friend or a loved one. Each massage can be tailored to the needs of the individual, so prepare to relax.

The signature treatment at this spa is the Turquoise Wrap, which is based on the Native American belief that turquoise is a protective color and creates a sense of peace and well-being. The wrap begins with a gentle exfoliation using Hopi blue cornmeal, followed by a warm, ionized turquoise clay wrap. During the wrap, a rain-stick ritual is used with essential oils aimed at cleansing the spirit. Following a shower, a full-body honey mask is applied. You will then enjoy a steam to hydrate your body.

If you want to visit an impressive spa with world-class service, you will not be disappointed at Golden Door.

- Featured treatments: Turquoise Wrap, Ritual-for-Two Massage
- 10% discount
- Hours: Daily 9:00 AM–7:00 PM

Golden Door Spa

ACKNOWLEDGMENTS

Thank you to all the spa owners, managers, directors, and therapists throughout Colorado. Without your wealth of knowledge, this book would not have been possible.

We sincerely appreciate all of the guidance from Fulcrum Publishing and especially the editing expertise of Katie Wensuc and Shannon Hassan.

We would like to recognize Jan Archuleta for the contribution of her artwork.

Special thanks also to the following people who provided extra information for the book and were not acknowledged in the text: Mandy McManis of Castle Rock, Colorado; Kimah McCarty at Chipeta Sun Lodge & Spa; Maggy Dunphy, Julie Goraj, and Angie Magee at Aria Spa & Club; Katie Coakley and Sacha Kostick at Allegria Spa; and Jamie Carothers and Shalane Vashaw at Coldwater Creek: The Spa.

Spa Etiquette

Arrive at least 15 to 20 minutes before your treatment.

Communicate with your therapist before and during your services about your comfort level and needs.

Inform your therapist of any health concerns you have so he or she can provide the best service for you.

Leave technology behind—turn off all electronics.

Inquire about the spa's cancellation policy.

Choose the option that is most comfortable for you when deciding whether or not to leave on undergarments.

Some spas include gratuity with the services. If not, 15 to 20 percent gratuities are customary.

Ask for a female or male therapist if you have a preference.

Let the therapist know if you choose to talk or not.

Take your bathing suit and other fitness clothes along in case you partake in other activities offered at the spa.

Drink lots of water!

SPA TRENDS

Partnerships between spas and communities are providing educational programs that are focused on overall healthy lifestyles.

Spas are becoming increasingly more environmentally conscious—many offer organic product lines and are enhancing the efficiency of their heating and cooling systems.

Spas are incorporating organic foods as a part of their cuisine offerings.

Spas are integrating Eastern and Western techniques, such as Thai massage, Watsu, and even a combination of yoga and Pilates known as yogalates.

Massage sessions are being incorporated into the workplace, offering employees an opportunity to relax during the workday.

Medi-spas are on the rise as consumers find more options to alter their appearance without having surgery.

Hospital spas are offering patients spa treatments done bedside.

Airport spas are providing quick massages, nail-care services, and even oxygen therapy for travelers.

Mobile spas will come to you, offering services in the convenience of your own home.

Spas are catering to male customers by creating men's locker rooms and lounge areas.

Spa Glossary

Acupressure: Integrates the use of specific pressure points to support energy flow in the body during massage treatments.

Aromatherapy: Uses essential oils therapeutically during massage and body wrap treatments.

Ashiatsu: A deep massage where the therapist walks on the back of the client. It improves the client's posture.

Ayurvedic: An Eastern Indian philosophy that incorporates the science of life with medicinal herbs and oils to maintain balance and support skin on a cellular level.

Banya therapy: A steam therapy that stimulates circulation and strengthens the immune system through the use of high heat and brushing the body with oak leaves.

Body brushing: Use of a dry brush to remove dead skin and improve circulation.

Chakra: The idea of opening seven energy centers throughout the body to maintain wellness and balance.

Craniosacral massage: Works the layers between the skull and the brain to relieve tension and create better energy flow.

Day spa: Offers professional spa services during the day.

Deep-tissue massage: Works with all three layers of muscles to relieve chronic pain. (This type of massage is not recommended for everyone.)

Destination spa: Offers educational and fitness programs along with spa services that enhance healthy lifestyles. Often provides on-site overnight accommodations.

European facial: Includes deep cleansing and moisturizing of the face along with a neck, shoulder, and face massage.

Floatation: Integrates ideas of buoyancy in a capsule-shaped tank to relieve tension in the body.

Hot-stone massage: Uses warm stones strategically placed along the body to allow the healing properties of the stones to be absorbed and relax the client.

LaStone: Uses warm and cold stones to stimulate circulation and promote relaxation.

Myofascial release: Linked to treatments that involve manipulating the connective tissue between muscles. Often uses stretching and pulling.

Raindrop therapy: Energetic alignment that incorporates nine essential oils during the massage to help restore balance.

Reflexology: Founded on the belief that pressing specific areas of the feet, hands, or ears can have therapeutic benefits and reveal information about what is happening in the body.

Reiki: A technique that is based on energy work to reduce stress. Not a massage.

Resort spa: Professional spa services located within a hotel or resort. Often includes fitness programs.

Rolfing: Manipulates soft tissues and involves stretching and pulling to help improve posture and the effects of gravity on the body. Based on the work of Dr. Ida Rolf.

Sensory therapy: Awakens the five senses.

Swedish massage: Combines long, smooth strokes to improve circulation, flexibility, and relieve muscle pain. Uses a lighter touch than that of deep-tissue massage.

Thai massage: Opens up energy flow through stretching. Often done on a mat. Loose clothing should be worn.

Thalassotherapy: Uses sea products to detoxify, exfoliate, hydrate, and balance the skin's pH levels.

Vichy shower: Often used during wraps to rinse off scrubs. Usually the water showers down from a jet above so the client does not have to get up from the massage table.

Vita-Flex: Reflexive massage based on the electrical circuitry of the body.

Water dance: Similar to Watsu, but the client is taken beneath the surface of the water.

Watsu: Conducted by flowing dancelike movements in a pool where the body is supported by the therapist and the water.

ADDITIONAL RESOURCES

Book
The Colorado Guide by Bruce Caughey and Dean
    Winstanley

Websites
Annaé Geoceuticals: www.annaebeauty.com
Myofascial therapy: www.drlowe.com/myofascial/
    generalinfo/myofthrpy.htm
Floatation tank information: www.floatforhealth.net
The Real Essentials: www.therealessentials.com/
    vitaflex.html
The Rolf Institute of Structural Integration: www.rolf
    .org/about/index.htm

About the Authors

Kalpana G. Muetz

has been teaching and designing courses for Regis University for the past seven years. She has a master of arts in liberal studies and is currently completing a doctorate in adult and post-secondary education. She is engaged in several academic and freelance writing projects. Muetz has lived in Colorado for over fifteen years and, with her love of the outdoors, has experienced much of what the state has to offer. Spa-going is a great balance to her very active lifestyle. She and her husband live in Bailey with their twin daughters.

Kristi L. Frush, EdD,

has been teaching writing, research, and adult education for seven years. She currently teaches at both Regis University and Colorado State University. Frush is a fourth-generation Coloradan. In *Colorado Spas*, she combines her love of Colorado with her love of writing. She has been frequenting spas for over fifteen years and enjoys the stress relief they bring to her busy life. Frush resides in Highlands Ranch with her husband and their two children.

Jillian LaVigne

possesses a bachelor's degree in English literature and composition with a minor in art history. She is currently engaged in several creative writing and fine art projects. She has worked as an editor for newsletters in the ski industry and for a glass company. She has written in many different arenas, including skiing, home design, and energy conservation. LaVigne practices yoga and meditation for relaxation. Visiting spas is an extension of this meditative practice for her. LaVigne lives in North Denver with her family.